BATFISHING

IN THE

RAINFOREST

Books by Randy Wayne White

Sanibel Flats

Batfishing in the Rainforest

The Heat Islands

Man Who Invented Florida

Captiva

North of Havana

BATFISHING

IN THE

RAINFOREST

—

Strange Tales of Travel & Fishing

—

Randy Wayne White

THE LYONS PRESS

Contents

Introduction 1

ON THE LAND

The Legend 11

Sweat Shop 19

The Boys of Autumn 27

Crocodiles at Home 49

New Mexico Connection 57

The Swamp Ape 63

They Shall Inherit 83

Hanoi Jane Goes to Shooting School 91

ON THE WATER

How to Be a Competent Southern Waterperson 101

The Big Book 109

Coming to America 117

Lessons in White-Water Style 131

Navy SEALs 139

The Great Equalizers 147

The Outward Bound Mutiny 155

The Best Tarpon Fisherman in Singapore 167

ON THE ROAD

Curse of the Artifact Hunters 177

Guatemala, Guatemala 183

The Strange Mammals of Ningaloo 191

The Sickness of Peru 203

To Say the Tiger's Name 219

Jumping with the Polar Bears 225

Batfishing in the Rain Forest 235

Introduction

Most of the stories in this collection were written during a period of time when I was a light-tackle fishing guide at Tarpon Bay Marina on Sanibel Island, Florida. None of the stories takes place at Tarpon Bay; only a few make even a peripheral mention of fishing—yet there is a connection. To understand the connection, you must first learn a little about Tarpon Bay.

Tarpon Bay was a type of marina once known in the South as a "fish camp," which is to say the facility was long established, the bay was shallow, buildings were sun bleached, and the docks were wobbly. Also, the marina sold fish—fresh, cooked, and frozen. Out back of the marina office, where mangroves shaded the water, there was a commercial scale and a cleaning table. Pelicans and egrets liked to stand on that table, waiting for handouts.

Tarpon Bay was not like the concrete and corrugated marinas preferred by government code enforcers—which is probably why it was such a popular place. Dockage for small boats could be had at a price, and there was a waiting list. Joyce, the deep-fry cook, made the best conch sandwich on the islands, so at lunchtime, the traffic in the dusty parking lot was as noisy as the patrons were enthusiastic. Because Tarpon Bay Marina looked the way it looked—crooked docks, the bay, small boats, mangroves, and bleached wood—it attracted artists too; artists not just of the heart, but also of the hand and the eye. These artists would set up their easels on the docks, mix their paints, and try to capture the look of the place. A very few actually captured the *feel* of the place; a rare occurrence that drew personal congratulations even from the marina's fishing guides—not that we fishing guides were snobs, or even stingy with praise. It was just that, to congratulate anyone, we had to leave our shady lunch spots. Spend 300 days a year on the water, in the Florida sun, and your standards in art will sharpen even if your appreciation for art does not.

Tarpon Bay Marina did have its own feel. All good marinas do— and there are fewer and fewer good marinas. A good marina comprises more than the sum of its docks, bait tanks, and ship's store. A marina is an ephemeral community as intricately linked as any coral colony, and with a personality flavored, more or less, by each of the individuals who form it. Some marinas are as friendly as stray dogs, some are grumpy and aggressive, and some are as uninteresting as the corporations that own them. You would have to ask a Tarpon Bay client how friendly we were, but I can say for certain that the marina was never uninteresting.

Tarpon Bay Marina was dominated by its proprietor, Mack. Mack was a big man partial to Cuban cigars and plantation hats, and he did everything with bold strokes and a capitalistic flourish. Mack made a lot of money as a banker, retired when banking lost its charm, and took a flyer on a marina. "Where free enterprise is just a little freer," Mack was fond of saying. He loved money—no, he loved the rituals involved with making money. Offer Mack a chance to bargain, an opportunity to dicker, and he would drop even the most compelling task to try and beat you down a dollar or two. Oh hell, Mack did love money. He didn't lie about it, and I shouldn't either. Hundreds of times in the years that I was at the marina, Mack looked up from the ringing cash register, winked, and said, "They're playing my song."

Mack was a good businessman, but he was more than that too. Mack had hobbies. He enjoyed gambling and fishing, and he dabbled in antiques and art. He collected paintings of clowns—everyone on the island knew that. But what few knew was that Mack's collection of clowns extended into his own work corps. If you were a plain, honest, hardworking lug, you didn't have much chance of being hired by Mack. But if you had some personality quirk, if your interests ranged beyond snook fishing, if your sense of humor was more liberal than your politics, then Mack probably had a job for you. Among the personalities who made up the marina community were Willie, an 80-year-old German refugee, whose bad temper was exacerbated by low blood pressure and a stint in the Nazi youth corps; Graeme, who left his New Zealand home at 16 to travel the world before settling on Sanibel where, for many years, he wooed a fascinating variety of women and worked—despite the fact that he was in the country illegally; and Nick, who was smart and hardworking, but who stuttered so badly that he was incomprehensible on the telephone.

So what did Mack do?

He put Willie in charge of the rental boats, which meant that, on a daily basis, Willie dealt with dozens of amateur boaters under the most maddening of circumstances. "Mister!" we could hear Willie yell from the docks at some bewildered rookie, "Don't aim dah damn motor, steer it! It's a boat, not a gun!"

He put Nick in charge of answering the phone in the fish market. Invariably, the caller's first question was about variety, and we would all hold our breath while Nick replied by rote, "Grouper, sna-na-napper, flounder, sea trout, cah-cah-cobia, shark, and . . . da-dol-dah-da-dol-da-dah . . . *maui maui.*"

He made Graeme, the illegal alien, marina manager, which meant that it was Graeme's responsibility to deal with all the petty, self-important government officials that a marina invariably attracts. Graeme

3

had roamed the world and knew many things, so ineffectual bureaucrats were hardly a challenge. Mack loved the irony of that, relished
the private knowledge that the same people who would have scram-
bled to have Graeme deported (had they only known) were not in
Graeme's intellectual ballpark. "Take it easy on them," Mack would
say kindly, "there's a reason they work for the government."

Tarpon Bay Marina was not a mean-spirited place; indeed, it was
usually amiable and always cordial. But if you could not laugh at yourself, it was not a place to linger. When Mack was once bested in a business deal, we began calling him "Top Dollar," for he had paid top
dollar for some piece of junk. He loved the nickname, and he always
smiled a little when he heard it, so we called him that for years. Among
the marina family, Nick was not embarrassed about his stutter, and we
all pulled openly for him when he was on the phone. Year by year he
became more confident so, on those occasions when he informed a caller, "And we have da-dah-dol-da-dah . . . DOLPHIN," the caller probably wondered why there was wild applause in the background.

As for Willie, his humor never much improved—but then, no one
really expected it to.

We fishing guides certainly weren't spared. Young guides are prone
to haughtiness so, to keep us in our places, Mack would sometimes tell
new clients outlandish stories of what they could expect to catch with
us—and then laugh at their dejected expressions when we returned
with 14-inch sea trout instead of the blue marlin and giant tuna he had
promised (but that do not frequent the waters around Sanibel Island).

During my years at Tarpon Bay, I was also trying to be a writer,
which Mack and Graeme and the rest well knew, so they offered en-
couragement when they could. Fishing guides are not easy to get in
touch with. We are usually out netting bait before first light, fishing
until noon, back on the water at one, and not finished at the cleaning
table until well after five. At a busy marina, that is the schedule—and
I sometimes fished that schedule for more than 40 consecutive days
without pause. Which is good for a guide, but bad for a writer, because

editors cannot call you when you are in a boat chasing fish. So the few editors who were interested in my work made it a point to call the marina during my lunch hour. On those rare occasions when they called, Mack or Graeme would unfailingly page me over the public-address system, even though I was right outside the door. I'm sure the editors heard them: "Paging Captain White, Captain Randy White, you have another damn call from New York," which was a kind attempt to make me sound more important—and more in demand—that I actually was.

When I received that page, I did not tarry—and not just because I was desperate for writing jobs, though I was. I hustled in because once, when I lingered, I arrived at the marina office to hear Mack telling an important editor, "Randy's not going to cover the America's Cup for you or anybody else until he gets these goddamn mullet gutted."

I worked at Tarpon Bay Marina as a fishing guide for nearly 11 years, several thousand charters. And I would probably be guiding there still if a few low-rung bureaucrats hadn't decided to close the marina not only to power boats, but also to fishing guides. Never mind that most guides don't tear up grass flats because they rarely go aground. Never mind that most guides are fanatical about game laws. Never mind that most fishing guides put on a daily workshop on the proper way to release fish—a tutorial that pyramids through all fishing society via our clients. The bureaucrats, even though they were trying to do their best, couldn't understand this and, in the end, it didn't matter.

As Mack would say, "Take it easy on them. There's a reason they work for the government."

It's been a couple of years since the marina closed, but the influence it exerted on our lives is still felt by most of us. Graeme has sailed on to the Virgin Islands, where he finds the massive charter operation he runs almost as challenging as the name of the region in which he lives. Nick still stutters, but he does so as a confident young father and manager of a successful business. The other Tarpon Bay fishing guides, Alex and Neville, are busier than ever working out of a neighboring marina.

But not all of us are still around to feel the influence of Tarpon Bay. Willie passed away without once making peace with a rental boat operator—not that anyone really expected him to. What we also didn't expect was that Mack, during a night of wagering at the greyhound races, would suffer a massive heart attack and die. But he did. The only thing about it that wasn't surprising was that Mack went out a big winner, payoffs on a couple of rich trifectas folded lovingly in his money clip.

So what does all of this have to do with this collection of stories? In high school, most of us learned that astronomers, by calculating the paths of known bodies, could deduce the existence of unknown and unseen planets. Well, in these stories, Tarpon Bay Marina is the unseen planet; the molding gravitational force that may not have shaped the stories, but certainly had an influence. More than one of these pieces was finished in a rush at 5 a.m. so that I could get it into the mailbox and then hustle to the marina to start catching bait for the day's charter. More than one of these pieces arrived in Chicago or New York with the grease stains from one of Joyce's conch sandwiches still fresh on it.

The marina also provided me with my biggest advantage as a traveler: No matter where I went, no matter who I encountered, I could introduce myself as a fishing guide and enjoy a warmer welcome than most writers could expect—or deserve. People naturally trust and empathize with a fisherman. I don't know why that is true, but it is. People quite rightly think that a guy who would travel halfway around the world in search of a fish—a fish he probably won't catch anyway—not only deserves their help, but, by God, *requires* it.

And they were usually right.

Tarpon Bay Marina is never mentioned once in any of these stories, but you will see little bursts of it here and there, bright proofs of its strong orbit; and you will sense that orbit in the strangest of places: on a pro baseball diamond; ducking gunfire in the mountains of Peru; bringing refugees out of Cuba; dog mushing in Alaska; training with Navy SEALs in California; fishing for bats in Central America.

I took leave from my job as a guide to do all of these things and more, and a little bit of the marina always traveled with me, exerting its influence, helping to organize the myriad threads of my life into one bright filament. It is for that reason that this book is dedicated to Mack and Graeme and the rest of the old Tarpon Bay Marina community, with additional thanks to those few editors, such as Terry McDonell and John Rasmus, who took the time to call at lunch.

The ordinary traveller, who never goes off the beaten route, and who on this beaten route is carried by others, without himself doing anything or risking anything, does not need to show much more initiative and intelligence than an express package.

THEODORE ROOSEVELT
from THROUGH THE BRAZILIAN WILDERNESS, 1920

ON THE
LAND

The Legend

Once, visiting the Key West docks, I struck up a conversation with a shrimper, a true Conch, which is to say he talked through his nose and wore white rubber boots. When I told him where I lived—a coastal town more than 400 miles away by highway—he said, "Hey now, you ever heared about that dog what they got up there?"

Dog?

"Yeah, that *there* dog. Dog can swim underwater and bring up cement blocks. Whole ones, from 15 feet a water, then swim them back to shore. Big brown curly lab. And understands *words*. Say this dog can swim down fish; catch them, too. Catches snook, reds; even a shark once. A friend of mine was talking it around the docks. An ol' boy he knew knows somebody what'd seen it. Man, I'd love to have one a his pups."

The shrimper thought I might know something about the stories, me being from the town where this dog was said to live, and that led us into a discussion of other dogs; dogs that neither of us had really encountered, but had heard much about. The shrimper told me the story of the grouper boat cocker that had twice saved all hands: once by leading them to a fire in the dunnage box; another time by waking them when the anchor broke during a storm. Then he told me about the shrimp boat golden retriever that had dived overboard and drowned itself the trip after her owner was drowned. The golden, the shrimper told me, had a 200-word vocabulary and knew the days of the week. It was a great loss felt by all.

I had already heard both of these stories in various forms, and the shrimper had probably already heard my story about the feral hog that had killed 27 catch dogs but was finally brought down by a collie-rottweiler mix, and about the pit bull from LaBelle who would sink its teeth into moving truck tires and flop around and around until the truck stopped. All regions have their legendary dogs, and it has been my experience that outdoor people collect those stories, knowingly or not, perhaps because dogs, unlike people, are still safe harbors for exaggeration. We can tell the wildest tales about animals we have never met, absolutely fearless in the certainty that our wonder and our admiration will never be dashed by a "60 Minutes" exposé or Senate subcommittee hearings. That people are human is a reality now beyond escape; that dogs are not makes them, perhaps, the last stronghold of legend.

The shrimper wanted to know about the dog in my town; the dog that could retrieve cement blocks and outswim fish. The animal that understood *words*. But instead of telling the man the truth, I told him what he wanted to hear because, while I had not propagated the legend, I was, necessarily, through association and loyalty, another of its protectors. And I did know the truth. The dog he was describing was once my dog.

○ ○ ○

I called him Gator because that's the animal he most resembled while in the water, and, like the reptile, he possessed certain quirks of character not normally ascribed to creatures allowed outside a zoo, let alone welcomed into a house. He was not a lab, though I often hear him called that. He was a Chesapeake Bay retriever, seven months old when I got him from an Everglades hunting guide, and already the subject of dark rumors, though I did not know it at the time. A wealthy northern client had given him to the guide as a present, but the guide, who favored tall pointers and catch dogs, didn't know what to do with him. He kept him in a run with his pit bulls until the Chesapeake— then called Wolf because of his yellow eyes—opened the carotid artery of one of his prize bitches. The guide decided to try and sell the dog and, if that didn't work, he'd shoot the damn thing and burn the papers. All this, I heard later.

Coincidentally, I had recently ended an 11-year association with a nice setter and was casting around for a new breed to try. Most people who like dogs have some vague mental list of breeds they admire and, at that time, I was leaning toward border collies, flat-coated retrievers, or a nice mixed breed from the humane society. See, the difficulty in choosing a good dog now is that some of the great breeds have suffered at the hands of pet store puppy factories and certain lowlife bench show fanatics who have bred only for confirmation or cash flow, and I did not want one of their mindless, hyperactive progeny. It was then that I happened to read a newspaper article about a Chesapeake Bay retriever that had, according to eyewitnesses, leaped into a flooded creek and pulled out a drowning child.

I liked that.

I had one very young son with another on the way, and we lived on a creek. I began to research the breed—just as anyone contemplating dog ownership should. There were relatively few registered Chesapeakes in the country (little chance of overbreeding), and only the most generous of souls would describe them as pretty (of no interest to the puppy factories). Everything I read I liked so, after having the dog x-rayed for hip dysplasia, and after listening patiently while the guide insisted the dog had championship bloodlines (I've yet to see a registered dog that didn't), Gator ended up in my home.

Every dog I have ever owned learned the basic obedience commands—to sit, to stay, to heel, and to come—after about four weeks of short daily training sessions. Gator took twice that long, but once he learned something, it was as if it had been etched in stone—an appropriate metaphor, considering his intellect. The dog was no Mensa candidate, but the commands he did learn he carried out like a Marine. What I didn't have to teach him was how to get things out of the water. Water was to Gator what air is to birds. On land, he might lose himself in the mangroves (more than once) or run into walls (often), but water transformed him into a fluid being; a graceful creature on a transcendent mission. The mission was simple: There were things in the creek—*many things*—that needed to be brought out. Our backyard became a littered mess of barnacled branches, shells, and other flotsam, even though each exit from the creek required that he latch his paws over the lip of a stone wall and then haul himself over, an exercise much like a pull-up. Since the dog did these pull-ups hundreds of times a day, month after month, his chest and forearms, quite naturally, became massive. Freakishly large. And, as the dog grew, so did the size of the things he retrieved. Tree branches became whole tree limbs. Shells became rocks—big rocks—for the dog learned early on that if the creek's surface was sometimes bare, the creek's bottom always held treasure. On a flood tide, the water was 7-feet deep and murky, but it made no difference. He would dive down and hunt and hunt until I thought surely a real gator had taken him, only to reappear 20 yards away, a rock or a limb in his mouth.

One morning I was sitting on the stoop reading when I noticed a neighbor's Boston Whaler drifting pilotless toward our property. I thought this odd until I realized my dog was towing it home. He had chewed the lines free with his teeth, and an emergency survey of other mooring lines in the area provided strong evidence that, had I accepted the Whaler, a 30-foot Chris Craft would soon follow.

At some juncture during that era of boat thievery, four more things occurred that enhanced his already growing reputation in the region: He dove underwater and retrieved his first cement block, he caught his first fish, he jumped through a second-story window to attack a pit bull, and he got an ear infection. Swimming the block ashore didn't surprise me, though the stranger who had come asking to see the dog and then threw the block seemed genuinely shocked. Catching the fish did surprise me, because I had watched Gator sit on the dock studying waking fish, only to dive and miss them year after year. Finally, though, he did manage to stun and swim one down, and he brought it to me, his tail wagging mildly (a mad display of emotion for that dog); a 10-pound jack crevalle that swam strongly away when I released it. The ear infection was a more subtle touch. It required an operation that left the dog's head listing slightly to the left, and people who came to see him would say things like, "See there? He knows we're talking about him, and he's trying to understand," for the tilt did lend an air of rakish intellect to an otherwise blank expression.

Added to all of this were Gator's all-too-often public displays of his own dark nature. Spending his earliest months in a run with pit bulls had left him with a mean-spirited view of dogs in general and of pit bulls in particular. I could take him jogging on free heel, and he never looked at another dog. But if one strayed onto the property, bad things happened. We were moving into a new stilthouse when a big pit bull came trotting into the yard, giving great ceremony to the decision of where to pee. I had been warned about this dog. He had free rein of the neighborhood, terrorizing pets and children, and the owners would do nothing. Gator was on the upstairs porch, watching with me through the screened window ... and then, suddenly, he was no longer there. It took me a long dull moment to understand what had happened, looking through the broken screen as Gator, making an odd chirping sound because the fall had knocked the wind out of him, attacked the pit bull. Gator accompanied the pit bull home, which is where the pit bull stayed—once his stitches were removed and he was released from the animal hospital.

I consider what my Chesapeake did that afternoon less an act of bravery than just one more demonstration that certain basic concepts—the effects of gravity, for instance—were utterly beyond him. I don't doubt for a moment that he would have dived into a flooded creek to pull out a drowning child. But he would have gone in just as quickly to rescue a log or a Subaru. We love to attribute to animals those noble qualities we lack, though often long for, in ourselves. But Gator wasn't noble; he was only pure of purpose. Other dogs suffered unhappy encounters with him. A few deserving people suffered too.

Once a burly lawman I did not know arrived at the house in a van. With the barest of introductions, the lawman told me loudly that he did not believe the stories he'd heard about my dog, but he'd come to see for himself. Then, as if to underline his contempt for exaggeration, he slid open the van's side door and two big Doberman pinschers jumped out—inexcusable behavior on the lawman's part, but that's exactly what he did.

Gator was in the creek tearing out mangroves when he wind-scented the Dobermans, and he came charging over the bank, blowing water from his nose and roaring; roaring because that was the only noise he could make with a tree limb in his mouth. The Dobermans were too stunned by this draconic vision to move and so fared badly in Gator's attack from the sea. The lawman could move, but moving was exactly the wrong thing to do, which is why Gator turned his attention to the lawman, who was trying feverishly to drag his two dogs back into the van. The lawman left, making threats out the van window. My dog had bitten him, and also injured two trained police dogs. I would hear from the authorities, he promised. And he kept his promise.

The next day, a squad car pulled into the drive followed by a van from animal control. They wanted to see my dog. I whistled for Gator, and he came trotting around the corner carrying, to my surprise, a 20-pound hammerhead I had been dissecting on the dock. From inside the animal control van, I heard one of the men say, "Holy Lord, he kills sharks, too. I'm not getting out."

But the men did get out. They watched Gator retrieve bird dummies. They watched him retrieve the cement block. They saw how he worked on hand signals. And when Gator had finished doing all this, one of the men said, "See how he tilts his head when we talk? It's like he understands what we're saying. Man, I'd love to have one a this dog's pups."

Gator's reputation spread.

Television stations sometimes called to see if I would allow them to do a piece on Gator (always refused) just as the friends of friends sometimes stopped to watch the dog who swam underwater and caught sharks. More than once, in those years, I heard a stranger describe my own dog to me with details as wondrous as they were exaggerated.

But, in reality, Gator was probably not much different from dogs you have known or owned. He was a good dog, which is to say he minded well, and he was mine. When I got up to leave the room, he followed. He was good with the boys, didn't yap, didn't hump, didn't whine, didn't eat the furniture, didn't jump up on strangers unless he meant to bite them, only stole the one boat unless you count canoes, and he wouldn't have gone for the cavalry if I had waited a year.

He wasn't an overly affectionate dog, either. He liked to have his ears scratched, but I can remember only one time in our nine years that he actually licked me. I had given up hunting because I simply took no joy anymore in killing for sport those same animals I loved to watch while on the water or in the field. But I had made that decision, I saw now, without giving any thought to the dog I had trained exactly for that purpose. I had, I realized too late, defected, in a small way, to the ranks of bad breeders and bench show fanatics by robbing another working dog of its heritage.

So I decided to give hunting one more try. I loaded Gator and shotgun into the boat and ran the tidal creek to a saw-grass marsh where, I knew, there were brackish ponds that held scaup and mallards. It would have been a bad day for fishing anyway, but it was a fine day for ducks: February gray and windy, with sea fog over the bay. Gator felt good, I could tell. He kept his ears perked like a puppy, and his yellow eyes glowed, and I wondered, *How can he know?*

It had been years since we had hunted together. But now, as then, he understood that this was not just a boat ride. This was not playtime. Cement blocks and sunken logs were meaningless; swimming before a shot was fired, unforgivable. This, he knew, was *work*.

I positioned him at the water's edge, but close enough so that my left hand could reach his ears, and we waited. I missed two easy shots before I finally took a single—a mallard drake—and Gator vibrated beneath my hand, listening for the release, *Bird!,* before sliding into the water, throwing a wake in the dark chop as he found the mallard and pivoted as if equipped with a keel. I watched him swimming toward me, that big brown tilted head and those eyes. He should have brought the bird to my feet and then sat, but he didn't. He couldn't. His hips were ruined by disease, and he licked my hand as I scooped him up, telling me that it hurt when I held him that way, but there was only one alternative, and that would soon come.

I carried Gator back to the boat and placed him on the deck by my feet. Then I drove the legend homeward, toward his rendezvous with 9 ccs of pentobarbital, and the grave I had already dug for him.

Sweat Shop

ying bare-ass naked on a table in a tiled room, my attention was naturally drawn to the man who approached me carrying a bucket of coarse salt and a length of garden hose.

"Something about this procedure strikes me as a little strange," I told him as he affixed the hose to a spigot protruding from the wall.

"Me too, at first," he replied, placing the bucket on the table, "but after a couple hundred times, you get used to it."

Fat chance, but I was in no position to argue.

Strange procedures go on in this country daily, the best and worst of them bubbling out of municipal orifices such as L.A. and New York to commingle with this republic's mainstream. Those that are widely embraced become fashion, those that are not become trends. Living in the 1990s, a decade in which trends are more fashionable than fashion and fashion is eschewed by the trendy, I find that staying apace is not easy. Vigilance is requisite; participation obligatory. Which is why I happened to be lying naked on a table at Safety Harbor Spa & Fitness

Center, which is generally considered one of the best and trendiest facilities of its kind in Florida and, perhaps, the whole East.

"We've got to hose you down," the man, whose name was Greg, said. "Wash off all those body poisons. Then we use the salt; rub it on real good. Then we use the loofah."

My God, I thought. Not the loofah.

My body poisons had had a tough enough time of it. Earlier that morning, I had been given a Shiatsu treatment: a full hour of acupressure, which, according to the attendant, should help detoxify my system through steady, gentle pressure on my energy zones—a Homeric undertaking, considering my life-style. The attendant was not intimidated, warning, "In that case, don't be surprised if you have to spend a lot of time in the toilet later. That's how my first treatment affected me."

Which added a certain drama to the procedure that followed: the herbal wrap. I was wrapped in towels freshly removed from a vat of boiling herbs and left to steam for 20 minutes—a variation of the Colonel Sanders recipe, which the new attendant, Roger, said was really a treatment handed down from the American Indians. "We use 20 different kind of herbs," he told me. "They help draw out impurities."

Now I was in for what Safety Harbor literature calls the loofah saltglow rub, and I felt as if my body was dangerously low on poisons. But to join the trendy, one must not only prevail, one must also endure.

Greg, the loofah attendant, hosed me with the same diligence one might hose a Jeep Wagoneer in preparation for a wax job, then glopped handfuls of sea salt onto my body and began to rub.

It should be pointed out that certain men—immature men who have yet to come to terms with their own masculinity—may find themselves cringing at the touch of a loofah mitten controlled by the hand of another man. For these stunted souls, relaxed, intelligent conversation might help relieve their irrational uneasiness, as well as stem a hellish sweating from the ears that they may experience.

I remarked to Greg, "How about those damn Miami Dolphins, huh? Are they having a season or what? *Hell!*"

Greg said, "Ah . . . right. See, what the salt does is, it removes all the dead skin. I'm not hurting you, am I?"

"Me, hurt? Oh hell, no. I mean, when you think about what those football players go through. Hard asses, man. Quality personnel. I love guys like that. . . . Geesus, wait a minute. I mean, I don't really *love* them——."

Greg said, "After I finish with the salt, I'll use the loofah mitten to apply a Savon cleansing gel. That will take all the impurities off your skin."

"What I mean is, I like guys like that. I mean, I used to play football. I mean, they're guys—like me. Like us, I mean."

Greg said, "Then I'll put on a Lancôme skin conditioner; it's supposed to make your skin real smooth. Kinda soft, too."

"When I think about some of the bizarre stuff we used to do—the other football players used to do. Nobody could love a football player. Hah! Not me, that's for sure."

Greg said, "Another ten minutes, and we're all done."

"Football players," I confided to Greg, "are scum."

The loofah rub wasn't bad, really. In fact, once I got used to it, I liked it. Back in my plush room, I checked my skin in the mirror. Greg was right. I looked real smooth and shiny. Damned if I wasn't getting what enthusiasts call that health-spa glow.

○ ○ ○

The health-spa glow has never been uncommon among the rich and trendy, but these days it is being seen in outdoorsy types and athletes too. There's a reason for that. A generation ago, spas were known colloquially as fat farms; a place where soft people with money could go to be pampered while suffering caloric restraint. But the health-spa industry, no stranger to trends, has been broadening its base in recent years by appealing to aerobic freaks and other fitness buffs.

As Hannelore Leavy, vice-president of marketing for Spa-Finders, a New York booking agency for spa vacations, told me, "The world of spas has changed enormously in the last few years. We represent more than 300 spas worldwide, and many of those have changed their emphasis to weight loss through fitness. They're not starving their guests anymore. They're using education about nutrition and fitness; giving guests something to take home with them. People can still go to lose weight, but now they're offered so much more. Name a recreational interest, and we can find a spa to suit it."

Leavy also told me that the proliferation of spas across the country has put many within the reach of a middle-income budget. "We represent spas that charge $4,000 or more a week, but the average is more like $1,200, and some run less than $100 a night. It's now a vacation that almost anyone can afford."

Well, advertising people know how to make things seem more attractive than they sometimes are, so I decided to try a spa myself. There are nearly 200 spas in North America. All but the cornbelt states seem to have at least one. I could have chosen one of the luxury spas, such as the Golden Door in Escondido, California, or Canyon Ranch in Tucson, or one of the much less expensive new-age spas, such as New Life Holistic Health Retreat in Pennsylvania or the Lotus Center for Health in Virginia. But I settled upon Safety Harbor Spa & Fitness Center, just west of Tampa, because its prices seemed mid-range for the industry (about $500 for a three-day package), and because it offered a program for dilettante triathletes such as myself.

Safety Harbor, on Tampa Bay, is one of Florida's oldest spas; a huge place on its own grounds built around a great white main house that branches off into an equally large complex of exercise rooms, pools, saunas, and a boxing training center (Mark Breland, Henry Tillman, Gary Mason, and other world-class boxers train here).

Upon my arrival, I was shown to my room, then given an orientation tour by assistant manager Tom Nurse, who, as an outdoor sports enthusiast, told me he was enjoying playing a part in transforming the place from an old-time spa into a "center for health through nutrition and fitness."

"It's kind of funny," Nurse said, "but in the old days here, guests used to order what they wanted, then the waiters would bring them what they thought they should have. 'No, you can't have the pasta; you've already had your calorie allotment for the day!' That sort of thing. Now, instead of prices on the menu, we list the calories for each dish and let our guests make their own decisions. Same with classes. We offer more than 30 workout classes a day, plus educational sessions. They can take all the classes they want, or they can have us design a special program for them, or they can lie by the pool all day."

"You can't impose health," Nurse told me. "It's a personal decision."

○ ○ ○

After spending my first day getting blood tests in the spa's medical center, and after being herbal sweated, acupressured, kneaded, and salt treated, my personal decision was to track down a six-pack of Coors and rehydrate with some much-missed poisons. But first I ate dinner in the elegant dining room (the venison osso buco, a sassy little entree at 320 calories, was excellent). Then the woman at the desk told me, yes, the spa had a cocktail lounge—a dark place behind the stairs where, I discovered one's footsteps echo as they might in a Nebraska savings and loan.

It was after 7 p.m., yet only the bartender was there, and he seemed both pleased and surprised to have a customer. "First beer I've sold all day," he explained. "I don't do a lot of business down here, but the place will start jumping pretty soon."

"Late cocktail hour?" I suggested.

"No, that's when we put out the baked apples and the fruit juice. Everybody's hungry by then."

The bar never did jump, but it did twitch for a short time. I met a lot of fellow guests, all of whom were congenial, though a few seemed genuinely nonplussed that I was drinking a beer. "My God," said one woman, "he's the same man I saw eating pie at dinner!" Which is exactly the kind of comment that has started more than one tragic pie fight, though I spared the woman when I later passed her in the dining room.

Generally, guests I met during my days at the spa fell into two broad categories: those who bitched and whined about how much better spas were in the old days, and those who were passionately in favor of the new fitness approach. I gravitated toward the latter group not only because I feel whiners should be permanently herbal wrapped, but because I had a great time at Safety Harbor.

Triathlon instructor Tracey Wetzel helped me tailor a workout schedule that complemented my inabilities. I have done maybe a half dozen of the short-course triathlons, always finishing way back in the pack (which I don't mind) and long after local restaurants have stopped offering breakfast (which I do mind). I told Wetzel that I wanted to get faster not because I served to win, but because I wanted to finish in time to be served. He empathized and created a schedule for me.

I tried some of the exercise classes too. The advanced aerobics session was a killer—bouncing around to music in a mirrored room beside women who, in their striped tights, looked as if they had been kidnapped by a circus. Which is an attractive thing to picture, unless one is in there with them, trying hard not to sweat or make unattractive noises or collapse in a defeated heap on the floor, unable to keep up. Which I couldn't. That's why I didn't take many classes.

In the evenings, I ate dinner at what the waitress called the "party" table which is where they seated people who had come to the spa alone. The party table was a fun spot; a lot of hooting and tittering went on over gourmet food. I met several stockbrokers, physicians, and lawyers, and heard more about New York politics than can be good for the digestion. One woman told me the reason she takes spa vacations is because it is one of the few ways she can get away from her surgical practice without leaving the country.

"I love my work, but the daily life-and-death pressure can hammer you physically and emotionally. For a time, I thought I'd go off the deep end. But then I found out about spas, and it's changed my life."

Safety Harbor Spa & Fitness Center didn't change my life. But I did come away from those few days feeling more rested and refreshed than any traditional vacation has ever left me. I ran every morning, then swam and lifted and biked. I don't know if I lost weight, because I didn't check. I consulted with Wetzel in the evenings, and we made certain adjustments in my workout schedule.

To train full time, with a personal coach, is among life's few self-indulgent acts that one can enjoy without guilt or regret. It's a rare thing; makes one feel righteous. Like you've earned a few beers. Like you don't need to smack people in the face with pies, even though they deserve it. Kind of like the loofah rub, it leaves you with a nice kind of glow.

The Boys of Autumn

I t is two hours before Florida's Senior Professional Baseball Association's inaugural game, and though fans are already arriving at Fort Myers's Terry Park, and though Pompano's Gold Coast Suns are taking batting practice, and though all sorts of other interesting things are going on, I am watching Luis Tiant. Tiant, grinning like a kid in his blue Gold Coast uniform, is clearly enjoying his first opening day in seven years, but more than his mood is buoyant. Still exchanging barbs with his teammates, Tiant duck-walks to the fence and begins to dispense his morning coffee or soda or whatever through the chain link, the rakish sweep of his hips adding a boyish flair to his voiding. One of the ground crew, a polite man named Reynaldo, is also watching and, in Spanish, reminds Tiant there are rest rooms available, just like in the major leagues. But Tiant only waves Reynaldo closer and begins to charm him with the story of how, when playing for the Red Sox, he once placed this *pinga* of his in a bun, covered it with condiments, confronted his manager, and said, "You call anymore morning meetings, skip, I give you a bite of this!"

Sitting in the dugout with manager Earl Weaver, Tiant would watch the hosting Fort Myers team defeat his club 13-0 in a game riper with proprieties than drama. Commissioner Curt Flood helped welcome the crowd of 2,300 while the PA announcer pointed out that camera crews from both CNN and CBS were in attendance. Connie Mack, Jr., son of the baseball legend, threw out the first ball, which, the announcer said, would be immediately jetted to Cooperstown for enshrinement in the Hall of Fame (though, a month later, the ball still had not arrived at Cooperstown and, as curator Peter Clark observed, "If we had it, we might actually use it, but you can't display what you don't have.").

This same announcer, perhaps unnerved by so much history, then introduced the Fort Myers Sun Sox as the Sun *Sets,* a blooper only those of us sitting in uniform in the Fort Myers bull pen seemed to catch. "That's us, boys, the Sun Sets," said outfielder Rick Manning. "Now let's totter out there and knock their knobs in the dirt"—a quote that mirrors nicely the game face attitude not only of Manning, but of the other 216 players, managers, and coaches in the eight-team league who took to fields around the state that day.

In Orlando, U. L. Washington drove in two runs to beat Clete Boyer's Bradenton Explorers 3-1. In Winter Haven, the St. Petersburg Pelicans beat the Super Sox 9-2, despite the stratagems of Bill Lee, 42-year-old manager, pitcher, outfielder and designated Lao-tze spokesman. In West Palm Beach, Dick Williams's Tropics beat Graig Nettles's St. Lucie Legends 8-1. And in Fort Myers, pitchers Dennis Leonard, Steve Luebber, and Don Hood shared the shutout, while teammates such as Dan Driessen, Marty Castillo, Amos Otis, and Tim Ireland combined for 14 hits—the first of their 13 runs italicized by a directive to Tiant from the Sun Sox bull pen: "Bite that, Louie! Bite *that!*"

What most fans thought they saw that opening day was pitchers throwing 80 to 90 mph fastballs, infielders performing with the sweet deliberation of snipers, and outfielders making diving catches despite pulled hamstrings.

But many sportscasters and reporters saw things differently, taking strange refuge, perhaps, in the sacred aphorisms of baseball's establishment: If the idea is new, it can't be good; if the players are old, they must be bad. A reporter from Baltimore said that the quality of play was far inferior to that of the major leagues, then took the dichotomous route, adding that, still, it was amusing to watch 38-year-old outfielder Cesar Cedeno throw the ball 300 feet on a line to home plate. About the players, a reporter from Boston concluded, "Their participation shows a disrespect for the game they're supposed to love."

It could be argued that these reporters communicated what they expected to see rather than what they actually saw, but for one lone derisive thread: lack of foot speed on the field. As one person in the press box put it, "They're hobbling around out there like old men." Which was true—but rather than serving as evidence that the league was a joke, it was precisely this odd hobbling gait that was the key indicator that something extraordinary was about to take place on the playing fields of Florida's old Grapefruit League circuit. With only two weeks to get in shape before opening day, nearly half the league's position players went into their first games with pulled hamstrings, yet they continued to play with an intensity unexpected in light of their injuries and the relatively low pay ($6,000 to $36,000 for the season). Returned to the very fields upon which most of them, as young men, had proven themselves worthy of the major leagues—the same fields that, in later spring training games, would be party to their banishment—they had now been given an opportunity to take seriously, as players, the skills they had spent lifetimes developing and to take a second shot at the game that had, over the years, taken so many shots at them.

Strange ingredients were entangled that day; odd portents, such as a 49-year-old man whizzing in foul territory and the die-behind-the-wheel play on the field, yet many in the media focused curious venom on the players' lack of speed rather than seeing the significance of their refusal to brake. As one reporter said, "Just about any ex-high school player over the age of 35, who's stayed in shape, done some running, could play in this league. It's strictly amateur class."

Though I had been with the Sun Sets only a short time, no one was better qualified to judge how absurdly wrong he was, or had more reason to wish that he was at least a little right—because, unknowingly, the would-be player he described was me.

○ ○ ○

When founder of the Senior Professional Baseball Association (SPBA) Jim Morley sat down with his fellow investors and, together, they drew up the bylaws, they left a loophole those of us never gifted enough to play pro ball could have driven a no-cut contract through. The loophole was this: "Each team can have up to three non-former major leaguers on its regular roster." A number of reasons are given for this curious lapse, the most plausible of which is that the owners, worried about the availability of quality middle infielders and catchers, wanted the option of drawing from the talent pool of ex-triple-A players. But the clause says nothing about ex-triple-A players or even professional players. It simply reads "non-former major leaguers," which, in fact, includes a whole generation of balding, middle-aged, weak-armed former high school jocks, few of whom were actually dull enough to think they had a shot at making one of the eight SPBA teams—but I take pride in having tried anyway.

My baseball history is important only in that it reflects the histories of so many. Perhaps it mirrors yours. I played the game from age eight through high school, was invited to a lone major league tryout camp at which I received a thanks-for-coming but nothing more. I played four or five more years in rank leagues before finally giving up the game that had long since given up on me. But once one has played baseball with serious intent—however limited one's physical abilities—cutting the cerebral ties is not so easy. In strange towns, I see the lights of a ballpark and I am drawn to them. If it is a baseball game, I stay and watch. If it is softball, I'm on my way. If I drive by a Little League game and the pitcher has a nice release, I'm there for at least an inning. If there's a kid with a sweet swing, I'm good for two, maybe three. I've never jogged alone past a baseball diamond in my life without rounding the bases, and if I find a ball in the yard, I must pick it up and do what we all did thousands of times as children: throw it onto the slanted roof and make the catch that saves the game. To say I love baseball is too strong. I've never followed major league box scores or collected baseball cards, and my store of baseball trivia is weak. But even though it has been 15 years since I last played, the game itself still exerts a strange pull on me; has an almost gravitational influence so, like a planet at perigee, I seem locked in a deteriorating orbit at the center of which are fixed odors and elements: the sensory dynamics of mown grass, red clay, wood, and glove leather, crude jokes, liniment, old men with cigars, and the lunate haze of a ballpark at night, like moon glow.

The day I heard nonprofessionals could play in the over-35 league was the day I began calling for a tryout. My rationale, though flawed, was simple: Few major leaguers, judging from the Old Timers' games I had seen, exited into civilian life as fitness freaks, nor did many of them appear prissy about weight control. It seemed plausible that I could do now what I had been unable to do 20 years ago: beat one of them out of a position.

I ended up speaking with Pat Dobson, manager of the Fort Myers Sun Sox and also a pitching coach for the Padres. Dobson does not look like most baseball managers of fact; he looks instead like a manager designed in Hollywood: tall, articulate, lean with the Clint Eastwood habit of lowering his head slightly when talking so that he peers up and out at you. On that first meeting in the clubhouse, though, he did little peering at me; he seemed busy and preoccupied until I mentioned that, when not trying out for baseball teams, I made my living as a fishing guide. Suddenly I had his attention. Light-tackle fishing guide? Yes, I told him—for 12 years. Dobson, it turned out, is a passionate fisherman and, after a discussion of tides and baits, decided maybe I could have my tryout after all. Which is why, for 29 games, I was able to join the team—if not as an actual member, then at least as a peripheral party who was able to dress out, catch in the bull pen and, on those occasions when Dobson remembered I was not around just to talk about the habits of littoral fishes, take batting practice.

It would be inaccurate to suggest I had a chance of making the 24-man list of activated players—a fact obvious even to me after my first day on the field. That partition of chain-link screen, I quickly learned, does more than separate the diamond from the bleachers; it separates, as well, the fantasies of the stands from the more strident realities of the playing field. For a time, I nursed slim hopes of making the taxi squad as an emergency catcher. But as those hopes also faded, I contented myself with hanging with the team as long as I could, enjoying the cramped bus rides, the motel beer sessions, and sitting in the bull pen during the games, where I filled five small memo books with the notes that follow.

FIRST WEEK (At Home; St. Lucie Legends vs. Sun Sets)   Home is Fort Myers in Lee County, once a country backwater of palms and Southern charm that has now been all but absorbed by the influx of Midwesterners who have, in the last 20 years, transformed the towns of south Florida into a chain of Kokomos-on-the-Gulf, creating the illusion that Florida is, in fact, the North's southernmost state. But Lee County has had the foresight to preserve many of its small-town landmarks, one of which is Terry Park. Nearly each year since 1923, major league baseball has come to this small stadium with its green bleachers tiered beneath a tin rain roof, bringing its entourage of baseball legends, teenage phenoms, and big-city news jocks who come to cover spring training in the Grapefruit League. From 1923 to 1935, the Philadelphia Athletics trained here, followed by the Indians, the Pirates, and the Kansas City Royals. The base paths, laid down nearly 70 years ago, have carried Ty Cobb, Tris Speaker, Ruth, DiMaggio, Mantle, Clemente, Yastrzemski, Brett, and Bo Jackson. Terry Park, its infield tended like an Augusta putting green, is one of the few remaining antique ball yards on the old Grapefruit League circuit.

My first day with the team, I arrived five hours before game time not only because I was anxious to get on the field, but because I didn't want to come in when the clubhouse was full and have to react to what I feared would be 27 faces staring silently at me, wondering who in the hell was this new guy? So I arrived at 2 for a 7 p.m. game to find the clubhouse already more than half full, guys lounging around in sliding shorts, reading the paper, but instead of stares I got brief smiles in greeting. As I found my locker and began to change, Tom Spencer, a former Indians outfielder, came up to me and asked, "Do you play?" For a moment, I thought he was asking if I played baseball—it seemed extraordinary that they could spot me as a fraud so quickly. But then he added, "Bridge, I mean. We need a fourth." At a table behind him, Marty Castillo, a catcher, and pitcher Rick Waits looked on as I said I didn't know anything about bridge, at which Castillo grimaced and said, "Ah great—so now we've got another guy not worth a shit. Who the hell's in charge of acquisitions around here?"

This was my introduction to the Fort Myers Sun Sets. Never once was I asked where I had played ball or even if I had played—though that all came out later in conversations in the bull pen. To men who had spent much of their professional lives moving from team to team, and who were accustomed to arriving at the clubhouse to find a teammate's locker cleaned out with a different name taped above it, no unfamiliar face was a surprise to them, nor even cause for much curiosity. I would be the new guy for a few days. Then, hopefully, I would become one of the guys. And then, when management decided it didn't need me, I'd become the guy who was here for awhile but didn't make it, the one who didn't play bridge. In a business that is essentially nomadic and filled with small comings and goings, the only constants are the game itself and life in the clubhouse, which is perhaps why many of these once-retired players are to be found in the clubhouse far earlier than required—some even on off days. As outfielder Larry Harlow told me, "On game days, you don't have time to really do much at home, so you might as well come in early. And on off days—well, I hate off days. I've had too many of those already."

33

Harlow, nicknamed "Hawk" by the team, has worked in construction since 1981, when he was released by the California Angels.

○   ○   ○

The St. Lucie Legends are in town with their pinstriped blue and gray uniforms and list of big-name players: Graig Nettles, Bobby Bonds, George Foster, Jerry Grote, and Vida Blue, but they come in without a win, while the Sun Sets are 2-0 after sweeping Earl Weaver's Gold Coast Suns. After catching batting practice (BP), I hang around the cage to watch the Legends hit; watch Nettles and Bonds both lofting home runs over Terry Park's distant outfield fence (360 feet down each line), until something catches my eye through the nearly empty bleachers. I walk to the exit nearest the visitor's locker room and there, on the empty practice diamond, Vida Blue is sliding.

Sliding?

Yep, no doubt about it. He slides into second, then slides into third. Each time he pauses to inspect the dirt accumulating on his game pants. One of the grounds crew is also watching, and I wonder aloud why a pitcher would practice base running. The grounds crew guy grins and says, "Because Vida just wiped pine tar all over his leg. Now he's covering it up with dirt. But I'm not supposed to say anything because Vida said at this level it's not cheating, it's just getting an edge."

With occasional visits to the pine tar on his slide-savaged pants, plus his 90 mph fastball, Blue gives up only one run in five innings with the help of two circus catches by Juan Beniquez in center. We lose 8-1. Afterward, the normally cheerful clubhouse is grim. The sound of cleats echoes off the cement floor, and guys limp toward the showers wordlessly—most of them with huge hematomas on their thighs, the black badges of pulled hamstrings. Even Dan Driessen, who seems always to be smiling, is subdued.

For the first time, I realize how seriously these guys are taking their return to baseball, and how much they hate to lose.

This second game of the Legend series goes our way, though. Sitting in the bull pen with pitchers Don Hood, Eric Rasmussen, Doug Bird, Dennis Leonard, Dick Drago, Dave LaRoche, and Castillo (who has a night off from catching), we watch Otis hit a three-run homer in the first. Then Manning and Ireland each drive in runs in the second. Designated hitter Pat Putnam is hitting ropes on his way to a three-for-four night, and, defensively, Wayne Garland pitches five no-hit innings while third baseman Ron Jackson backhands balls, barehands balls, throws off his right foot, and makes it look easy. By the sixth we have a 9-1 lead and the mood in the bull pen, always relaxed, relaxes even more. Bird and Leonard, who played for the Royals when they trained at Terry Park, begin to talk about George Toma, K.C.'s famous groundskeeper.

"Remember when those guys started peeing in George's rain gauge? Man, they just about drove him nuts. George would come to the park and find four or five inches in the rain gauge every single morning. He'd look at that thing and scratch his head, then look at the parking lot to see if there were any puddles. No puddles. Then he'd carry the gauge around, show it to us and say, 'You know, it musta rained cats and dogs last night, but this dang field didn't hold a drop! Not a drop!' We'd just pull away, like *'Get that thing out of my face,'* and say, 'You're doing a great job, George. You're magic, man.'"

Which reminds one of the coaches of a joke played on Cleveland's Sam McDowell. "We took the hinges off Sam's hotel door one night, and he comes back after a long party, rams the key in the hole, and the whole door gives way. He falls into his room face first, right on top of the door, and just lays there groaning. Then he jumps up, goes straight to the phone, and calls the police. We're out in the hall, and we can hear him talking. 'This the police? Hey, somebody busted into my room. Yeah, no shit. I think they took my gun, too. A big gun.' The moment Sam mentions his gun, we clear out. We knew nobody had *touched* his gun. Then, next morning Sam goes for a swim in the hotel pool and drops a big log right there. People all around, and Sam drops a massive floater. Then he tries to blame it on some kid. I mean, the log's as big as the kid's leg, and he's trying to blame this eight-year-old. That night, Sam goes out and throws like a two-hitter; back when he threw *gas*. But in the clubhouse, he's still bitching about this kid he says dropped the big log."

As they talk, Harlow makes a long run and a diving catch, thudding shoulder first and skidding on his face past the foul line right in front of us. Castillo yells, "Way to hustle, Hawk; way to give it up!" Then to the bull pen he observes, "That's a tough way to get sober. I tried it in high school once."

We win 11-2, and we win the next night too, with solid defensive play from Harlow, Castillo, Driessen, and utility man Kim Allen. Walking from the bull pen to the locker room, Dick Drago studies the scoreboard, admiring the team total of 17 hits, and says with an appreciation that could be felt only by a pitcher, "My God, and we haven't even had time to cork our bats yet."

○ ○ ○

(ON THE BUS TO POMPANO)   Life at middle age may be essentially serious, but life in the Senior League, especially during a bus trip, is not. There are 33 of us sitting shoulder to shoulder on this air-conditioned motor coach; 33 grown men of varied antecedents, respected in their communities, some of whom haven't ridden a team bus in more than ten years, so there is a reunion atmosphere and the worn jokes, which seem as funny as ever, create a curious spatial vacuum in which time appears as warped as the humor.

In a seat ahead of me, a former Yankee pitcher is telling a story about Lou Piniella: "We were on the bus outside Yankee Stadium, getting ready to go to the airport when this girl jumps on, drops her pants, and wants all of us to autograph her butt. . . . "

From the back of the bus, pitcher Steve McCatty suddenly interrupts, groaning, "Aw no, Hose just cut the cheese!"

To which catcher Tim Hosley says immediately, "No sir, it wasn't me, man! It was Catty. He's the one smelled it first."

But the Piniella story continues: "Well, that sort of thing happens in the show, but we're gentlemen about it, and we all sign this girl's backside as she moves down the aisle. . . . "

McCatty, who looks like a muscular Captain Kangaroo, is moaning, "Aw Hose, something crawled up you and *died*," and Dan Driessen is spraying a can of Right Guard as air freshener, yet the story progresses.

"So Steinbrenner hears about this chick later, and he jumps us about it in the clubhouse, really pissed off. . . . "

Infielder Pepe Frias, who has the strange habit of repeating nearly everything he says three times, yells to Hosley in support, "Hose, man, you can fart, you can fart, you can *fart!* "

And the Piniella story ends: "So Piniella listens to this bullshit until he can't take it anymore, and says to Steinbrenner, "Aw George, if you'd been on the bus you'da signed her ass too.""

Sitting next to me is Rick SaBell, the only player without major league experience to make the team. SaBell played one season of Class A ball before the Pirates released him, and he has taken a leave of absence from his job with Continental Airlines, he says, not just because it's a chance to redeem what he perceives as his failure to make it in baseball, but because it's an opportunity to be part of a team again. He points out, correctly, that those of us on the bus have a generational tie: We all played Little League and high school ball at about the same time, but only those with exceptional gifts went on to play in the major leagues, leaving the rest of us behind.

"Just being on the taxi squad," he tells me, "it's an honor to be on the same field with these guys. At first I was worried I wouldn't be accepted because I never made it out of A ball. But they've been great to me; there's no snobbery at all, even from the big-name guys. There's nothing fake about it; no bullshit. They're just happy to have a chance to play again."

SaBell has not only been accepted, in many ways he is a pivotal figure in team unity. Because he is not tall (5′ 7″), looks like actor Joe Piscopo, and is also an airline flight attendant, many team jokes revolve around him. From the back of the bus, McCatty calls out, "Hey stewardess, we need more Diet Coke back here." Then: "Heads up, you guys, Piscopo's going for Coke. Get your knees out of the aisle or you'll break his nose."

Grinning, SaBell yells back, "Get your own Coke, you big dumb shit."

McCatty, who is also a color commentator for the Oakland A's, rises: "It's *Mister* big dumb shit to you."

Even players who just sit quietly are laughing, turning their faces toward the focus of hilarity: late-1960s expatriates who weathered Beatlemania and Vietnam without noticeable scars; faces that still have that weird boyish light, good timers released into the establishment but never ingested by it after a lifetime of bus trips on a road that this generation of baseball players thought ended long ago.

○ ○ ○

SECOND WEEK (Sun Sets vs. Gold Coast at Municipal Stadium, Pompano) We lost last night 7-6, despite a ninth-inning three-run homer by Otis, and this morning coach Tony Torchia has brought us early to this bleak old field for optional hitting. I hit first, then go to put on the catching gear, but Torchia surprises me by telling me to pitch instead.

I like pitching, but the guys seem to enjoy it even more, teeing off on my flat fastballs, hitting these screaming shots, some of which would surely kill me were it not for the screen from behind which I throw. The fourth or fifth hitter is Pepe Frias ("You can pitch, you can pitch, you can *pitch*!"), but we are interrupted by someone yelling from the home team's dugout: "What the fuck are you doing out here?"

I look to see a small man in a Gold Coast uniform marching toward me, and he says again, "What the fuck are you *doing* out here?"

Clearly, he is yelling at me, and in the confusion of the moment, I wonder if he is one of my disgruntled fishing clients. But then I realize the man is Earl Weaver, and assume he has spotted me as a non-pro player. Weaver stops at the mound and, wagging his finger at me, demands, "What are you guys doing out here so fucking early? We take BP first."

To add to the confusion, from home plate a voice with a Spanish accent is yelling, "Give me a peetch, man! Just one peetch!" and I look to see 54-year-old former Yankee Pedro Ramos, begging for one of my flat fastballs.

Weaver says, "You guys aren't fucking supposed to be out here yet!"

I can't tell if Weaver is actually angry, but just in case, I point to Frias in the batting cage and say, "It was his fucking idea—talk to him," figuring Frias will tell Weaver to bite it, bite it, *bite* it. As Weaver walks toward Frias, Ramos is still calling, "Just one peetch, man. Just one peetch!" and, to me, Weaver yells over his shoulder, "Christ, just throw him the fucking ball. It's the only thing that'll shut him up."

○ ○ ○

Standing at the batting cage, I watch a new pitcher trying out for Gold Coast. The pitcher is throwing to Paul Blair, and Weaver is calling to the pitcher, "Just toss it in nice 'n' easy, Jim. This is just BP, doesn't mean shit. This ain't your tryout." Blair hits a half dozen screamers, and Weaver yells, "Okay, Jim, now try a few curves. Just spin it up there; don't worry about it breaking. This doesn't mean diddly." Blair knocks the next two off the wall in left-center, and Weaver turns to the man standing next to him and confides, "Christ, this guy Jim can't throw a fucking curve ball either."

Batfishing in the Rainforest

$$\bigcirc \quad \bigcirc \quad \bigcirc$$

At night, this ragged Pompano field glows with a strange fluorescence. Before nearly empty stands (attendance 400), with palm trees rattling in a gusting sea wind, we beat Gold Coast 14-4, with Amos Otis (called A.O.) hitting his second and third consecutive three-run homers. Otis, 42, is having the best start of his professional career, hitting .455 with 17 RBIs in only seven games, and the baseball card collectors are waiting for him as he exits the locker room. But Otis's attention immediately swings toward three Little League–age boys who are at the park late and alone, still carrying their schoolbooks. He says to them: "You guys shouldn't be up so late. Your homework done? Open those books and let me see your homework. Hey . . . you better head straight home and get this work done—then get to bed!"

Otis's paternalism is not uncommon on a team—or in a league—where nearly every player is a father, but riding next to him on the darkened bus, I feel his concern for those kids come into sharper focus when he begins to talk about his relationship with his youngest son, Cory, 15.

"My last year in baseball, 1984, I was with the Pirates, hitting about 160, no home runs, and they released me midway through the season. Cory was just ten, but he remembers how it was. The Pirates told me I was released at the airport, getting ready to board for an away series. Seventeen years in the majors, and they tell me like that, me with my bags packed. So the last five years, the only baseball I played was with Cory. We'd play catch in the yard, and he'd tell me year in, year out I could still play. I'd say, 'Naw, Cory, I can't play no more.'

"When I got the opportunity to play here, I wanted to do good. That last season with the Pirates has always kind of been a thorn in my side; I just hated going out like that. Thing is, I had no idea how I'd do on the field. I didn't want to embarrass myself, but mostly I didn't want to embarrass my family. I think it was like that with a lot of guys." He grins. "So far, though, things are working out. Last night, I called home and Cory answered. He didn't say hello, how ya doin', nothing. All he says is, 'I told you you could still play, Dad. I *told* you.' "

○ ○ ○

THIRD WEEK (Sun Sets vs. Legends at St. Lucie Sports Complex)

One falls easily into the routine of baseball life on the road. After mornings spent jogging or giving Torchia fly-casting lessons, I take the bus to the park where we take BP, stretch, play long toss, then take infield. Because we arrive so far in advance of the game, there's plenty of idle time for the running jokes that are part of the fabric of this team and probably all teams. Tim Hosley, who is fearless on the field, has a horror of insects, so it is not unusual to see him being stalked by someone palming a freshly caught grasshopper. Castillo enjoys lunging for throws, slapping his glove to your head, and acting as if he has saved your life—a stunt he pulls on me almost daily now. "That woulda knocked your damn side doors off," he always says. It has gotten to the point where, if Castillo is near and the shadow of a bird passes by, I instinctively duck, fearing for my side doors. This afternoon I watched Castillo sneaking up on Putnam who, just before being attacked, jogged off smiling as if Castillo did not exist. Castillo turned toward me, hands on hips, and said, "Crap, now I've lost my Indian skills, too," in clear reference to the early criticism players in the league took from the media.

It is my impression that, while skill parity may be judged from the bleachers, the tools that constitute those skills can be appreciated only on the field itself. Castillo holds up a ball, says, "Let's play some," and we begin to back away, throwing easily, until we are about 50 yards apart. Castillo probably has the best arm on the team, perhaps the best arm in the league, and as he begins to throw harder, I am puzzled, as I have always been, by this strange phenomenon, the major league arm.

Castillo and I are about the same size and build, yet when he turns the ball loose, the ball jumps from his hand and rises, gathering velocity. It's the same playing catch with outfielders like Harlow, Bobby

Jones, or Champ Summers. It's as if there is some elemental transfer of power when they throw; as if, through some blessing at birth, their hands are conductors in a weird kinetic process by which the ball is infused with energy and nearly glows with a voltaic if temporary life. For those of us who do not have the gift, it is a real pisser.

Castillo's throw jumps toward me and my glove pops, emitting a slight searing sound, the whine of leather. I throw the ball back, hard, but the ball seems suffocated by friction, its trajectory collapsing as if a small parachute has been pulled.

Otis yells to me, "Hey man, put some color in that rainbow!"

Kim Allen strolls by, listening to gospel tapes on his Walkman. "You're choking the ball," he says. "Hold it higher in your fingers. Get on top of it."

My next throw seems better: The ball appears to rise slightly, a brief flicker of life. I call to Castillo, "Did that move any?"

Castillo grins and answers, "Yeah, it moved—from you to me," and guns the ball back.

Castillo, who played for Detroit from 1981 to 1985, was a hitting star in the 1984 World Series, but spent most of his career playing behind Lance Perish. Since Castillo is only 32 (minimum age for catchers in the SPBA), even some in the news media are beginning to wonder aloud why he is not still in the big leagues. As Glenn Miller, a reporter who covers baseball for a local paper and Gannett News Service, told me, "He not only could play in the majors, he's better than a lot of catchers playing there now."

Though tempted to ask Castillo about it, I have learned that discussing the circumstances of a player's release evokes a momentary uneasiness, a reaction of near embarrassment more commonly associated with the discussion of a failed marriage. In a game where even the greatest hitters succeed only 30 percent of the time, and where even the best teams win only slightly more than they lose, all terms and feelings relating to failure should be diluted into unimportance. After all, there are far more neurosurgeons than there are men who have played in the major leagues. Even so, a sense of having failed seems to be the inescapable terminus that binds all careers in pro baseball.

After being released from the Tigers, Castillo started a very profitable business but still found time to play ball—in a semi-pro league for no pay. "For the California Earthquakes," he tells me, "because my brother was manager and I knew I'd get to start every game."

○ ○ ○

We won last night 2-1 behind outstanding pitching from Rich Gale and Eric Rasmussen. Tonight, though, we lost 10-9, yet it was an extraordinary game, a pleasure to watch. Infielders Pepe Frias, Tim Ireland, and Ron Pruitt made all the sweet plays, and the hitting was even better. Otis homered in the first, the third, and the ninth, but Legends catcher Jerry Grote, 47, homered in the second and the bottom of the ninth to win. As Grote rounded the bases, people in the stands took up the chant, "*Jerry . . . Jerry . . . Jerry*"—and that is the most extraordinary thing of all. Though official attendance was listed at just over 400, I counted fewer than 200 faces in this huge Mets spring training complex, and their voices made a wild sound, echoing off the cement portals before thinning in the night wind.

On the bus trip home, though, there is no talk of low attendance— indeed, players seem unconcerned that, on this road trip, the average attendance was closer to 500 than the 2,500 that team owners say they need for the league to survive. The players seem focused only on the game, and little else matters—a purity of purpose that explains, at least in part, some of the great baseball I have seen these last three weeks. Magical plays are being made each night on the field, yet few are in the stands to witness them. Weeks later, Bill Lee (known as Spaceman when he pitched for Boston) would liken these games to a Zen discipline in which artists perform in an empty room.

Behind me on the bus, I hear snatches of conversations, soft one-liners:

" . . . Catty, did you see Grote's shoes? Christ, he musta pulled them out of the basement or something—they had cobwebs on them. They were fucking old Wilson *Kangaroos*!"

" . . . To be a manager in the minors, you have to know at least 27 four-letter words, and those 27 have to include 'horse's ass and 'you egg-sucking mother dog.' "

" . . . Somebody dumped greenies into the coffee, but nobody knew it. Even the coaches were banging around the dugout like a bunch of Chinamen gone looney."

" . . . Piscopo, hurry up in there, man! I gotta pee, gotta pee, gotta *pee*!"

" . . . A soldier boy is a hitter who just stands there with a bat on his shoulder. And a Baseball Jones—that's what *we* are."

" . . . Rasmussen's right. You have to be Bob Newhart to be a pitching coach in the show, because the league is filled with Mr. Carlins. . . . "

Ahead of me, pitcher Jim Slaton sits with his son Jon, 14, their heads together and laughing, traveling in their own private orb. I rise to get another beer, and Doug Bird holds up his empty can, saying, as I take it, "Man, it seems weird, doesn't it? Riding a bus again after all these years. . . . "

O O O

FOURTH WEEK (Sun Sets vs. St. Pete Pelicans at Al Lang Stadium) St. Petersburg, sometimes called Cathetersburg by people who know it only as a retirement center, is one of the best baseball towns in the state. Players who seemed not to notice the empty stands of Pompano and St. Lucie now seem caught in the party atmosphere of the 1960s rock 'n' roll being played over the PA and of stands already filling an hour before game time.

"Wild thing, you make my heart sing. . . . "

McCatty, who is using a fungo bat in the bull pen to give Hosley chipping lessons, looks up briefly and says to Rick Waits, "Man, don't you hate it when they play that song before you pitch?"

Waits just grins as the Troggs sing on *"You make everything . . . groovey."*

Beyond the lights of the stadium, the sky is iridescent: A moon rind rides a fading sunset, with Venus, a bright blue shard, suspended above. North of the moon I see a bird gliding on straight wings, and holler to Don Hood, "Hey Hoody—an eagle!" Hood, who is a serious amateur naturalist, stands beside me, watching, and says, "Great night to be at the ball yard, huh?" At that instant, a half dozen feral parrots scream past us, tumbling into the fronds of a palm tree. Pepe Frias sees the parrots and beams, for to him they must carry the scent of home.

Frias was born in the Dominican Republic village of Consuelo near San Pedro de Marcois, "The place where all the baseball players come from," he says. One of 14 children, he slept on the floor in his parents' house and quit school after the second grade to help support the family. But Frias had the gift of speed and the hands of a natural shortstop. At 16, he was chosen to play on his country's national team, and in 1967 he signed with the Giants for $1,500—money he gave to his parents before packing his clothes in a sack and leaving for spring training in the United States. But early in his first season, Frias broke his leg so badly that the Giants gave him his unconditional release, and he returned to the Dominican Republic thinking his baseball career was over. He was not yet 19. But then his mother hired a voodoo *shaman,* "a witch doctor," Frias says, to pray over his leg. "Three times she prayed," he says. "After she pray three times, my foot, it was healed. Three times, like magic."

For 12 years, Frias says, he played professional baseball in the United States. Released by the world champion Dodgers in 1981, he traveled to the Mexican League where he played and coached.

As I pick up my glove and head toward the bullpen, Frias yells after me, "Hey Rand! You can catch, you can catch, you can *catch.* . . . "

Batfishing in the Rainforest

O O O

Catching is what I like to do—though I am clearly out of my league here. The Sun Sets have Castillo, who is superb, plus Ron Pruitt and Hosley who, as Pat Dobson (called Dobber) says, "know how to win." This sounds like one of those meaningless old baseball chestnuts ("He came to play") until I talked with Putnam one day. After realizing, to our mutual surprise, that I had caught him in an amateur league game more than 15 years ago, Putnam went on to list the places he had played since: minor league ball, winter ball, eight years in the majors, then two years in Japan. Mentally, I tried to calculate the approximate number of games we had played since Little League. His total came to about 4,000, my own to just over 300. It would be roughly the same, we decided, for most pro players in the league. Counting practices, 4,000 games translates into tens of thousands of ground balls, fly balls, cuts at the plate, and complex game situations, which, to these men, must no longer seem complex. The game of baseball, which, to most of us, seems wonderful randomness caged between two foul lines, must, to them, reduce the world to its very sharpest focus. On the field, the options are obvious, and Dobson is right: They know what must be done to win.

I like catching batting practice. I like the way the mask tunnels your vision so that all that exists is the pitcher's eyes and the spinning ball. I like watching these guys hit, taking outside pitches to the opposite field, taking inside pitches deep, laughing and joking as they demonstrate a level of craftsmanship even they don't appreciate. Better than BP, though, I like catching in the bull pen. My first day, the pitchers seemed wary and made sure I heard their stories about pitching to enthusiastic amateurs: grim tales of split noses and broken teeth. We use no mask in the Sun Sets bull pen, but my face survived—probably because of the extraordinary control these guys have. Everything is in a box, knees to belt—the nasty curve balls, the sliders, and the forkballs with their weird spin. After a few games, left-hander Dave LaRoche would tell me, "The other pitchers and I were talking. You do a good job back there." An ego boost soon felled by Castillo who, a few nights later, would say, "Yeah, Randy, if we keep winning you might get a chance to play—if there's a real bad bus crash."

○ ○ ○

Rick Waits, who has allowed only one earned run in the last 23 innings, is pitching shutout baseball for us tonight, and everybody in the bull pen settles back because they know Waiters is after a complete game, and it looks as if he will get it. The St. Pete fans are really into it, yelling at the players, screaming at the umpires, making such a noise that people even ten blocks away must certainly know that baseball is being played here.

In the bull pen, one of the pitchers is saying, "Two a.m., and my wife and I would hear this banging on our door. I'd open it, and there'd be Piniella standing in nothing but his underwear, holding a baseball bat. He'd say, 'Hey, check out this stance. You see what I'm doing here? Tell me if it helps me get my hands out quicker.'"

Steve Luebber, who has been pitching very well in relief, follows my gaze to the statuesque and very pretty ball girl just down the foul line from us. We look at her, we look at each other, then look at her again. "My gosh," says Luebber, "looks like she stepped on an air hose, doesn't it?"

On the field, infielders who have supposedly lost their skills are putting on a fielding clinic, and hitters who have lost their eye are hitting ropes. More important, the fans are on every pitch, having a great time. At night, a baseball stadium filled with people takes on a life separate from the world around it, and this could be Shea or Candlestick or Fenway or Ebbets, but it's not, and it doesn't matter. The game is not only being played here, it is being played well; so well, in fact, that more and more people are agreeing that the Senior League was badly named. It should have been called the Masters.

Back at Terry Park one week later, with our record 16-5, Dobson would stop me in the clubhouse, and instead of asking about the feeding habits of tarpon, would tell me that the only way a non-pro player could make it in the league was if he could play all the positions. A real utility man. "But I have a scouting report on you," he would say, then proceed to give it: "Good defensively, hits with occasional power, can't throw for shit," which was not unlike a scouting report I had been given 20 years earlier.

In the weeks that followed, attendance around the league would pick up (though the league would later fail). Rick SaBell would be released (though another former Class A player, pitcher Steve Strickland, would make the team). Tim Ireland, who never got much of a chance in the majors, would go on a 24-game hitting tear and finally prove just how good he really is. Pepe Frias would become a home-crowd favorite, Amos Otis would continue hitting, and Dobson and Torchia, both gifted managers, would become acknowledged major league prospects. Yet the Sun Sets, plagued by pitching staff injuries, would begin a losing streak that would not end until some of the coldest weather in Florida's history ended.

On this balmy November night in St. Petersburg, though, with Waits pitching a shutout and the fans wild with purpose, all of that is weeks away.

Castillo, who has the night off, tosses me his catcher's glove and says, "There's no way Putnam has a better knuckle ball than me," and we go to the bull pen, where he begins to throw that strange pitch that brings the ball to life, drifting and diving, and my concentration is absolute as it floats through the lights as white as the moon and as round as the world.

7-0, we win again....

Crocodiles at Home

would have seen my first American crocodile several years ago if the photographer with whom I was traveling had not screamed, *"There's one!"* His shout of pure terror inspired addled wading birds to flight (I could see the birds banging around in the canopy of the tree I was trying to climb) and caused the croc to submerge, not to reappear.

We were canoeing the upper fringe of Florida Bay, the giant back-water of islands and grass banks that divides mainland Florida from the Florida Keys, which is the last protectory of this country's rarest of big reptiles: the saltwater croc. The northern boundary of the bay is, perhaps, the least-traveled water region in the state, and we had pad-dled most of the day along its monotonous vein-work of swamped mangroves when, halfway up a creek, I noticed an odd smell, like cow manure, then an elevated area: a clearing shaded by hardwood trees. I caught an overhanging limb and peered over the rim of the bank into the clearing. The place was one of those leafy caverns, all shadows and sun patches, ripe with egret skins.

Batfishing in the Rainforest

The photographer whispered, "Something lives here," which was obvious enough, though his tone communicated it better: "Something *dominant* lives here," which was my reading exactly. Even now I don't understand why I decided to get out of the canoe and have a look. It wasn't to impress the photographer—photographers cannot be impressed. It had more to do with the aura of that clearing. It was like coming upon a troll's den in the wilderness: a secret place that smelled bad and where bones were scattered everywhere. Who could resist?

I stood in the canoe long enough to convince myself the resident croc was not around, then set my sights on the far edge of the clearing where there was a tree big enough to support my weight. The farther I got from the canoe, the faster I walked toward the tree. Almost exactly midway between the canoe and the tree was a large mound of sand: a crocodile nest, I would learn later, but, feeling pressed for time, I didn't stop. That's when the photographer saw the croc, and that's when he yelled. No, he didn't yell. He screamed: "There's one!" To which I, already sprinting, must have called back, "Where?" for just as I leaped for the lowest limb—and missed—I heard: "The damn thing's right *there!*"

I don't know much about the American crocodile now; I knew even less then, for *Crocodylus acutus* is seldom written about and rarely seen. Almost everyone knows that Florida has alligators; very few know that, long before the Spaniards arrived, saltwater crocodiles inhabited the peninsula (though they were not described scientifically until 1869), and still inhabit remote regions of Florida Bay.

What little I knew of saltwater crocs came from reading about Nile crocodiles, which for centuries have added spice to beach sports, and visits to Australia where, in the northern territory, the animals feed on bush creatures and fish when they can't get a tourist. Once, when I was fishing for barramundi not far from Broome, a big croc surfaced within casting range of our little boat: a mindless-looking creature, all dragon's tail and teeth with sleepy slits for eyes that were black with purpose. If we hooked a fish, would he try to take it? I asked my guide.

"Only if he can't find a way to knock us out of this bloody boat first," the guide told me, then offered this humorous anecdote to illustrate: "A croc took a fisherman up Darwin way last month. Bit his head and shoulders off. Tourists tried to drive the damn thing off with sticks and stones. Funny, eh? Croc's name was Eric—at least, that's what the locals call it. 'Eric digested poor so-and-so.' Bloody odd name for a croc, if you ask me."

I had heard enough of these gruesome stories to actually go through newspaper files in Perth to see if the accounts were true. They were:

> The young American woman decided to go for a swim, and I was on the fly bridge of the boat, sort of keeping a look out. That's when I saw the croc. It was about five meters long and moving very fast. I yelled to the woman. She looked back and saw the croc and began to swim for the boat. We were all yelling for her to swim faster, swim faster, but the croc caught her from behind. It threw her up into the air, like a play thing, and swallowed her half way, feet first. The woman was looking at me when the croc took her under, just looking at me. She never opened her mouth to say a word. . . .

These were just two of the stories in my mind when the photographer yelled "There's one!" so it seems incredible that I missed that limb—it couldn't have been more than 10 or 11 feet off the ground. When I finally did manage to shimmy up the tree, the photographer and I got things sorted out, me hanging from the limb like a sloth as we called back and forth. Yes, he had seen a crocodile. It had surfaced right beside the canoe. Yes, it had scared him. Yes, it was big. Yes, it was gone now. No, I had found my way up the tree by myself and I could find my way down without his help.

After a mile or so of hard paddling, I had recovered sufficiently to exercise my right of indignation: Didn't the photographer know that, by yelling, he had ruined my chance to see the croc?—a mistake no serious observer of wildlife would ever make. The photographer's response was mealymouthed and mean-spirited: "If I ever meet a serious observer . . . different time zone . . . dispersion of sound waves at altitude . . . ass and elbows . . . " and other such lame remarks that don't bear parroting.

○ ○ ○

Recently, I told this story to Dr. Frank Mazzotti, a wildlife scientist who works in association with the University of Florida, Department of Wildlife and Range Scientists. Mazzotti is in charge of Florida's crocodile monitoring program, and the country's foremost expert on the species. Would I like another chance to see a croc in the wild, Mazzotti wanted to know? I could go out into Florida Bay with him and watch while he and his assistant checked the nests and maybe tagged a croc.

Would we be in a boat?

We would be in a boat.

I met Dr. Mazzotti and his assistant Laura Brandt late in the afternoon in one of Florida Bay's far backwaters. They had boated across from the ranger station at Key Largo; I had come by water from Flamingo. I transferred into their boat, and Mazzotti ran us even deeper into the backcountry, then dropped down off plane at the mouth of a creek marked by Styrofoam floats and a red marker that posted the area as a croc preserve, off limits to the public.

"The American crocodile is such a shy creature, and there are so few of them left, we want to make sure their nesting areas are as undisturbed as possible," Mazzotti said, explaining the buoys. "When I first started working on the croc project back in October of 1977, we counted 20 nests. Last year, we counted 29 and we know we didn't find them all. Part of that increase is probably due to the fact that we've gotten better at finding nests over the years, but we're still cautiously optimistic that the nesting population has increased slightly, or at least is stable. The nonhatchling population of crocodiles in Florida is approximately 300, so we're taking all the precautions we can to protect the species."

I told Mazzotti that I had never before heard anyone describe a crocodile as shy.

"In other parts of the world, crocodiles aren't shy. The Indo-Pacific crocodile of Australia and the Nile crocodile are both man-eaters. No doubt about it. But the American crocodile is not, even though it grows quite large. When going over the old accounts of Florida's earliest alligator hunters and poachers," Mazzotti said, "the one common thread is that everyone agreed that crocodiles are less aggressive than alligators. They have a well-established reputation among locals for being passive. In all the anecdotal accounts I've come across, I've heard of only one case of an American crocodile biting a man, and that was after some surveyors shot it and tried to catch it. With a few exceptions, crocodiles avoid people and places inhabited by people. Because of that, Florida's rapid growth is one of the greatest threats to the species."

Mazzotti idled us up the creek, which was only slightly wider than the 20-foot Whaler in which we rode, then tied off to the mangrove limbs when we came to an elevated clearing. There was a nest here he wanted to check. The nest was a heap of sand only a few meters from the water, crisscrossed with tail tracks; it looked active. Laura Brandt, who was working on her master's degree at Florida International University, got down on her knees and began to pull sand away. After several minutes, she carefully extracted an egg, large and ivory colored. It looked as if it were made of polished stone. "If we were doing an egg count," she told me, "I would mark this egg on the top to make sure it wasn't mistakenly rotated—that's very important. Rotating the egg kills the embryo. Then we would count the eggs and place them all back exactly as we had found them."

I was told that crocodiles lay their eggs—several dozen to a nest— in tight clutches. They lay in the spring and the eggs hatch in late summer, aided by the female croc. She stays close to the nest at hatching time and, when she hears the babies trying to break out, digs the sand away.

"You would expect the female to become slightly more aggressive at hatching time," Brandt said, "but that hasn't been my experience. Last summer we were out, and I was able to lift baby crocs right off the backs of their mothers without any trouble at all. If you want, you can come out with us later in the year and give it a try."

I told her that sounded fun—one of only a very few lies I told her that night.

After checking nests, we continued on up another even narrower creek that opened out into a massive brackish-water bay—lakes, they are called in south Florida—and waited for darkness. There was a two-man film crew with us doing a documentary on the Everglades for Boston PBS, and Mazzotti answered their questions as patiently as he had answered mine. Yes, at the turn of the century and later, alligator hunters had certainly killed crocs and sold their skins, but to what extent that damaged the population, he didn't know. In the 1920s, 1930s, and perhaps even later, crocs in the area were also captured and sold as exhibits. Now, though the population was small, it would hopefully stay stable as long as the integrity of Florida Bay was maintained— which was why the university's crocodile project had changed over recent years from research to monitoring. "The less we have to disturb the animals, the better we like it," he said. But it was still necessary to tag crocs and to keep track of active nests.

At sundown, we began our hunt. For Mazzotti and Brandt it was work; for me it was fun. The lake was shallow, spiked with old tree stumps, and I rode with them through the darkness utterly at ease in the knowledge that if we hit something, it not only wasn't my fault, it wasn't even my boat that would be ruined. Brandt held a spotlight on the bow, looking for reddish-yellow crocodile eyes, while Mazzotti somehow kept track of gray silhouettes, which he said were islands or points, an amazing navigational feat when you consider that the flare of the spotlight ruined, for me at least, all night vision.

Finally, Brandt spotted a pair of eyes—a croc, up on a mangrove bank, and Mazzotti had to ground the boat to get to it. The television crew had its filming lights on now, and I watched as Mazzotti, in that eerie white glow, climbed quietly out of the boat, stalked the animal, and finally caught it with a rope noose. There was a lot of thrashing and splashing; then he was wading back.

It was a small croc, about the size of a dachshund, with teeth like a cat. But it was a croc. While Brandt shaved the points off certain of its scutes (a marking code less harmful to the animal than an actual tag, I was told), Mazzotti made notes of its size, sex, temperature, and the salinity of the water. When the film crew had gotten all the footage it needed, and when all of the data had been collected, they let me touch the crocodile: rough skin warmer than the night air with bright eyes I had seen before; eyes still wild with purpose.

New Mexico Connection

I found a flute player among the black rocks of Albuquerque, New Mexico's West Mesa a few months ago, stilled in that familiar pose of a musician lost in his music: hips bent, head tilted, instrument pointed toward the earth, still playing after nearly a thousand years. There was a bird, too, on stilted legs. And a star. And a palm print. I touched my own hand to this stone etching—for that's what these things were, petroglyphs—and the sense of connection with its creator was as startling as anything I have experienced. The chasm of ten centuries was compressed by the thin membrane of fingertips, and it was like touching the hand of prehistoric man.

If there is an explanation for this, it has more to do with the nature of New Mexico's history and geology than the nature of my own lame sensibilities. Take the same short trip and you will understand. From Albuquerque, drive west across the Rio Grande, then north on Coors Boulevard to where Atrisco Drive climbs onto the low mesa which forms the city's western border. The great flexure of earth crust here is fringed by volcanic boulders—a sweeping black hedge of them, miles long, above which is the mesa plain, below which is the Rio Grande Valley. For thousands of years, the region's indigenous peoples climbed among this volcanic hedge in search of flat rock faces upon which to engrave the stick figures and eerie designs which, to many, now best symbolize those long gone cultures.

To see a photograph of a petroglyph is one thing. But to climb up over a West Mesa rock and come face to face with a solitary flutist is quite another. Behind you the Sandia Mountains jag toward the Monzano snow peaks, and the skyscrapers of downtown Albuquerque protrude through the valley's haze like crystal shards grown huge feeding on the mineral glitter of the Rio Grande. Even on a poor day, you have 40 miles of visibility, and the geologic theater of a continent shears away toward the horizon. New Mexico is a topographical guide to cataclysm: river tracks, wind sculptures, volcanic peaks; a red earth skin which has been torn, exploded, eroded and cracked by the epic convulsions of an evolving planet. It lies silent at your feet: the cicatrex of frantic geologic activity, of slow motion upheaval, so that, when viewed in the stillness of a desert wind, it almost seems that you can hear the grinding of rock against rock and the footfall of the petroglyph artist who hiked away just moments before your arrival. In terms of New Mexico's geological clock, the artist did, and that makes the sense of connecting even stronger. . . .

O O O

If one wishes to travel well, one must develop the skill of connecting well. This has nothing to do with catching plane A at X time. It has to do with finding a way to hack through the jumble of tourism garbage concerning the region we happen to be visiting so that we might best come face to face with the things which most interest us. This is not to say that data from a tourist bureau is bad. When one travels one is a tourist, like it or not. It can be argued, in fact, that we become tourists the day we leave the hospital as babies, so there should be no shame in assuming that role.

58

But tourist concessions are not always the best conduit, and by no means are they the only conduit to satisfying travel encounters. Let us say, for example, we are planning a vacation to the Caribbean and, in the course of our general pre-trip reading, we develop a mild interest in sea turtles. There are several well-documented accounts, we read, of green turtles being captured near a specific reef, transported over thousands of miles of open water, then escaping only to be recaptured months later having returned to that exact reef. Well, this is mysterious and wonderful, but we are tourists not biologists so, other than inviting a few vague observations from our travel guide, we spend our days parboiling on the beach and posing for snapshots—unless we have refined the craft of connecting well. If we have developed this most important of travel skills, the trip might go another way. Prior to leaving, we might call the biology department of a university where a string of more calls will lead us to their resident turtle expert. We will tell her the truth—that we are taking on vacation a new interest in turtles. I have yet to meet an expert in any field who is not happy to provide a beginner with guidance. She may not know anyone on the island to which we happen to be flying, but she certainly knows someone who knows someone. If that line of contact is followed with honesty and enthusiasm, and if we are lucky, instead of baking mindlessly on the beach, we might spend a day tagging after a turtle researcher or maybe a night in a bar with old turtle fishermen—connections few travel agencies offer.

This is exactly the kind of articulate, well-organized ground work that makes for memorable trips and best defines the travelers I most admire—but am almost always too confused, too *lost* to emulate. Yet even those of us who travel in a fog may connect well if we allow ourselves to be steered by the virtues of our interests. ("Say, can you tell me if I'm going north or south? Is this Monday or Friday? And do you know any old turtle fishermen?")

Persistence is the key here.

On my recent trip to New Mexico, it was exactly this combination of persistence and blind luck which led me to what could be a valuable contact for anyone traveling in New Mexico and, perhaps, the entire west: The Federal Bureau of Land Management. We all have our personal guidelines regarding intentionally contacting a government agency, and prior to my call to the BLM, mine were simple and conditional: If I received a Marine induction notice or was appointed Ambassador to France, only then would a call to a government employee be warranted. But because I was a stranger in Albuquerque, and because I knew no one who could give me a clear summary of the complex interweavings of the region's indigenous peoples, I found myself speaking to Anthony Lutonsky, archaeologist at the bureau's Albuquerque field office.

Lutonsky, who looks like a bronc rider with Ivy League antecedents, seemed genuinely happy to hear from a stranger interested in the area's prehistory. It had been his passion and profession for 16 years and the bureau welcomed amateur help, he told me. For more than twelve thousand years, he said, what is now New Mexico had been home or on the nomadic route of many groups of indigenous peoples (called Anasazis generically, though Anasazi also refers specifically to one of those groups), and visitors were encouraged to participate in their continued study.

"In just our management area, more than 11,500 Anasazi living sites have been catalogued, but we suspect there are 150,000 more which have not yet been discovered. There's just too much ground to cover and too few people. So we welcome volunteers. We're not a tourist agency, but if some person or group calls us and volunteers to go out looking, and if I know far enough in advance, I usually have time to meet with them, go over the topo maps, explain they're allowed strictly no-touch access, give them a BLM card and send them on their way." (Lutonsky can be reached at 505-761-4504.)

Would I like to go out looking? Lutonsky wanted to know.

That easy, the connection was made.

New Mexico Connection

○ ○ ○

Bruce Dyleski, a friend of Lutonsky's, was telling me a story that illustrates the fulminous, pervading quality of New Mexico's landscape better than any I have heard. Dyleski and I (Lutonsky had to work) were driving north out of Albuquerque toward the Rio Puerco valley, ascending through clumps of juniper herded on vast desert, when Dyleski pointed to a volcanic peak not far from the city. He said, "A few years back, some high school kids lugged a bunch of tires to the top of that peak. Then they set them on fire. You know how tires burn: black smoke came pouring out. There was a mild panic in Albuquerque. People thought the volcano was blowing again."

This is exactly the impression one gets hiking through the tumult of mesas, cerros, canyons and abrupt rock peaks: cataclysm formed this land, and only the brevity of our own lives creates the illusion that the rock towers are no longer collapsing, that the volcanoes are forever silent. Later, climbing with Dyleski up a crevasse of pulverized rock, I stopped in the silence and gloom of that stone wilderness, watching cloud shadows sail across 20 miles of bare valley, watching dust devils form, spin and collapse, sensing that, at any moment, the earth could shift again and crush us. Had I seen smoke coming from a distant black cone, I, too, would have been uneasy.

Dyleski, who is a local mountain bike and white water guide, said he knew of a remote stone fortress built by the Navajo on a crescent-shaped mesa, the walls of which rose 200 feet above the valley floor. But instead of approaching the structure from the mesa, as the BLM data suggested, we tried to climb from below and were stopped short at the precipice, though we could see the structure, its fitted stones blending into the natural wall. Then we tried to locate a well-known but seldom visited Anasazi site, but we couldn't find that either. Finally, in frustration, we set off at random and, atop the first cerro we ascended, stopped in the slow realization that we were not the first people to climb here. The ground was littered with pottery shards;

black painted designs on white masonry. They lay in the shadows of juniper bushes and in the pale sunlight, still bright after hundreds of years of dust and wind. We walked carefully among these artifacts, looking but not touching, like visitors at an art shop, yet there was a ghost town eeriness about the hilltop now, a sense of discovery and loss at once. To visit remnants of the mortal upon an earth canvas of the inexorable makes one feel tiny, very tiny, and as ephemeral as a swirl of dust. It touched in me that chord which urges we climb among rocks and leave something lasting. It provided a kinship with the petroglyphs we would later find, and the impulse which had perhaps created them: the longing to connect with things more permanent than the sound of our own step or the notes of a flute swept away by the wind....

The Swamp Ape

On the first leg of the Swamp Ape Expedition, G.M. insists that getting lost wasn't part of the bargain. When searching for a creature that probably doesn't exist, I tell him, one might as well be lost as not, but G.M. says nope, no way. That's why he wanted to follow main roads. That's why he brought a map. The map he produces from beneath his seat is the AAA-type, not the FAA-type—a selection I find troubling since we are not in G.M.'s pickup, but instead are at 2,000 feet in a small plane somewhere over the headlands of the Florida Everglades. "Gotta be an interstate around here someplace," says G.M.

I am reminded of my friend's uncle, B.D., a good-old-boy pilot who, when lost, circled water towers because towns often paint their names on water towers and B.D. could read as well as he could fly. B.D. over-aspired, however, and somehow memorized the route between Nassau and Fort Lauderdale, which is why he is doing 10 to 15 in a federal pen.

"Transportin' gandhi," B.D. would say—meaning ganja, not the Indian leader.

I've had my suspicions about G.M., too. G.M. dates a girl from Everglades City, where the Drug Enforcement Administration could have built an office for what it has spent on surveillance. G.M. speaks Spanish, lives on a sailboat, and believes in astrology as devoutly as he once believed in Jimmy Carter. He's also fond of quoting *Apocalypse Now*. This road-map business is not entirely unexpected, and I know we will be circling water towers before the day is done.

G.M. crumples the map and says, "Way I figure it, we're somewhere between Opa Locka and Fumbuck Egypt," which is his way of blaming me for wanting to cut cross-country.

There are a number of reasons why I do not want to fly the routes of main highways. The swamp ape has not been seen near a major highway in years, and the fact that I don't believe in the creature does not relieve us of the obligation of searching those areas where it *might* be found. That is, after all, the point of a Swamp Ape Expedition: to seek out places in the Glades where few others go—not with hopes of finding the beast, but with hopes of it leading us to regions seldom traveled and to people who, by virtue of being sympathetic to such a cause, reflect some of the weird qualities of the region itself. I've lived in the area for nearly 20 years, and while I've traveled the whole system, I'm not altogether sure I've understood what it was I was traveling over. Maybe few people have understood.

What I have to keep reminding myself is that the Everglades is more than a plain of saw grass where Dennis Weaver once used an airboat to chase Gentle Ben. The Everglades is, in reality, a huge biological unit of varied landscapes, and it includes nearly half the state, beginning just south of Orlando—where Florida settles slate-flat on a porous limestone base that tilts just enough to keep water flowing across it—and joins the wilderness outpost of Flamingo at the southernmost tip of the peninsula. The Everglades system encompasses 5,000 square miles, and I want to see it all—which is why this is the first time in our long friendship that I have finally agreed to set foot in G.M.'s ragged plane.

"You know what I don't trust?" G.M. confides to me. "I don't trust that coconut-headed customs guy in Belize. He's the one sold me these fuel gauges."

"Oh Lordy, Lordy," I reply, as G.M. banks to the west.

Soon, several small lakes come into view, glittering like ice fields down there among the tiny houses and palm trees. Where we are, it turns out, is in the central part of the state north of Lake Okeechobee. Sea World, Circus World, Cypress Gardens, and a dozen more tourist havens peel away beneath us, broad theme-park islands bridged by moving traffic. According to my maps—which I should have brought—a tiny body of water named Turkey Lake, just outside the boundaries of Disney World, is the northernmost link in the chain of lakes that feeds the Everglades, and it is something I would like to see. G.M. drops us to 1,000 feet, and there's the Disney World castle, pennants flying, a whole nation of motionless cars baking in the strata of heat between asphalt and sun. To the east are more lakes—one of them is certainly Turkey Lake—but I can't tell which. G.M. says what the hell, we're close enough to the headwaters and banks again, following what must be the Kissimmee River southward.

After a time we raise Lake Okeechobee, and to my surprise, there's an expanse of saw grass on its northern rim, through which the Kissimmee and several other small rivers flow. Then we are over the huge lake where, below, a bass boat trails a silver contrail and, beyond, are miles of cattle pasture and sugarcane, the soil looking as black and potent as gunpowder. I have read that these two industries—cattle and cane—are contributing to the chemical imbalance in the Glades that biologists say could spell disaster. The canals we see below, straight as conduit, transport megadoses of phosphate from cattle silage and nitrates from the cane-growing process directly into the Glades. I explain what little I know of this to G.M., who allows as how biologists are always complaining about something, and buzzes a line of Jamaican cane cutters, most of whom don't bother to look up or wave. G.M., who seems pleased with their nonreaction, says *"vets"* with misplaced pride.

We follow the main canal from Lake Okeechobee south, and within the hour there are flocks of white ibis rising beneath us, bright as flower petals against the brown saw grass. The land is empty, veined with creeks, pocked with cypress domes, eerie as a moonscape. Scattered across the saw grass itself are tear-shaped islands that show, in their contours, the direction of the watercourse, having been shaped over the centuries by its slow current. The islands all point southwest toward Flamingo and the Gulf of Mexico. I have stood in that saw grass for hours and not seen its water move, but here, in the shape of these islands, is proof: The river really does flow.

When the sign in Orlando welcomes you to the Magic Kingdom, it can be taken two ways.

O O O

In literature about the Everglades—and there's a ton of it—a point often made is that, to the observer, the region is more a cerebral pleasure than a visual delight. This theme in one stroke seems to recognize the delicate interdependencies of water and life, and at the same time apologize for the absence of mountains. There are no mountains, it is true. And because easy access to the Glades is limited, there's really not that much for the casual visitor to see. People arrive expecting a jungle and end up yawning over the miles of saw grass as they drive Tamiami Trail or Alligator Alley, the only two roads that cross that section of the state. Even the persistent usually must settle for a concessionaire's airboat ride or visits to Everglades National Park or Big Cypress National Preserve.

The Glades are flat, yes, but the "cerebral pleasure" theme is a bit deceptive. It ignores, for instance, the weird cast of the rugged, the lost, the imagined, and the mentally unsound who settled the region. Mixed bands of runaway slaves and Indians, mostly Muskogee and Creek, first came to the region as refugees and, beginning in 1835, endured a 20-plus-year assault by the U.S. Army that drove them into areas of the Glades where they never would have lived by choice, but where troops hell-bent on genocide could not follow. As a result, this mishmash of desperate, determined people became known, in the romantic lexicon of bad history, as the proud "Seminoles" that no army could defeat.

There were others, like Cyrus R. Teed, the Chicago physician who, while contemplating the expanses of sea and saw grass, realized in a flash that man lives on the inside of the earth, not the outside. The stars, he told his followers, were nothing more than uranium sparkles. Teed's group built their Garden of Eden on a river in southwest Florida and flourished until a bizarre sexual code (celibacy) depleted their ranks. There was also the tribe of nudists who settled northeast of Corkscrew Swamp with plans of interbreeding, hoping the progeny of their progeny would evolve into a master race, but failed because of bickering and the mosquitoes. This land on the fringe of civilization attracted others who existed on the fringe: a mobile community of cow hunters (Florida Cowboys), plume hunters, moonshiners, alligator poachers, murderers, and thieves, all of whom chose this region exactly for the qualities that repelled others. It was not a question of the land shaping the people, or the people shaping the land. Neither was hospitable from the start.

The only thing these people could not tolerate was civilization, and that arrived in 1928 with the opening of Tamiami Trail. Thousands of men using floating dredges had worked 13 years to complete the 120-mile road that connected Miami on the east coast with Naples on the west. Yet even this engineering marvel ended on a quirky note. The Miami road crew had built from the east, the Everglades City crew from the west, with plans of meeting in the middle. But their calculations were off, and, according to some workers, they missed badly—covering the mistake with a monstrous jag now called Forty Mile Bend. It was the last laugh the Glades would have for a long time.

Not only was Tamiami Trail a road, but it was an effective dam, and the grass river, with its flow interrupted, began to die, one interdependent link at a time. The logging companies came, laid tracks, and in less than 20 years shipped out an estimated 36,000 trainloads of raw cypress. The developers arrived in droves, like dark birds to carrion, and began massive dredge-and-fill projects that still threaten the survival of the Glades. Fortunately, conservation groups such as the Audubon Society interceded, brought political pressure to bear, and the carnage began to slow. In 1947, President Harry Truman, who had fished in Everglades City, said in his dedication of Everglades National Park: "Here is land, tranquil in its quiet beauty, serving not as the source of water but as the last receiver of it."

Under the tenancy of the National Park System and the eye of conservation watchdogs, the Everglades began a slow turn toward recovery, although its future is still uncertain. Private enterprise continues to threaten, and the Department of the Interior has been less than flawless in its stewardship. What did vanish with the appropriation of lands for the park was the cast of recluses and loonies who had mirrored the character of the area so accurately. Those who hadn't already left, or hadn't died, were booted out.

Through all of this, though, the swamp ape endured.

Searching for a swamp ape might be considered some chintzy metaphorical device for understanding the Everglades. Well, it is chintzy, and yeah, it's metaphorical, but it's more than that too. First off, there have been a lot of swamp ape sightings in Florida; so many that, in 1973, I began to keep a file. That file is now two files, and it contains dozens of eyewitness accounts. In 1974, north of Devils Garden, a little girl said she saw a baby swamp ape riding her tricycle, called her mother, and her mother saw it too. A St. Petersburg man claimed to be intimate with a swamp ape named Jim who loved salt and transistor radios. In June 1976, a sheriff's deputy in Grove City said one hissed at him as he held his spotlight on it. In September of the same year, a Buckingham man said he saw a creature that walked on two legs and smelled like burned sulfur, so he shot it seven times with a rifle. A Florida Yeti Research Society was formed in the early 1970s and began a heated debate with a state UFO society about whether the swamp ape was native to the Glades or came from outer space. In 1977 a state legislator introduced a bill prohibiting the molesting of "any arthropod or humanoid animal which is native to Florida, popularly known as the skunk ape." (The swamp ape is sometimes called skunk ape because it supposedly really stinks.) The Tamiami Trail village of Ochopee, which boasts America's smallest post office, held a Skunk Ape Festival, featuring a greased-pig chase and a pie-eating contest. As I collected these accounts, it seemed to me that the swamp ape was reuniting a segment of society that had taken the Everglades thousands of years of evolution to attract. But my files end abruptly in July 1977 with a sighting in the Florida Keys, of all places. Since that time I had not heard of another. Had the Everglades been tamed, or killed?

I had T-shirts made; I sent out invitations.

O O O

If it offers a chance to get off the beaten path, any excuse will be embraced by Peter Matthiessen. Matthiessen, a friend of mine and the author of *Wildlife in America, The Snow Leopard, Indian Country,* and other books of note, will search as cheerfully for a swamp ape as he will for things in which he believes. Not that he isn't open-minded. Matthiessen has been collecting bigfoot/yeti/swamp ape–type stories of his own while traveling the world, and he says he finds the evidence "interesting," if often inconclusive.

The search takes us to the tiny Everglades settlement of Pinecrest, located on a narrow road that loops off Tamiami Trail, then back again. Pinecrest once was a stronghold of moonshiners and poachers. Now the people who live here are a mixture of park rangers and those who choose to live or weekend in the Glades because they love the area. Matthiessen has been visiting Pinecrest for years and knows many of the people, but what he really comes to see is the wildlife. Already the trip has been a success for him. The previous day we traveled the Big Cypress by airboat with ranger Bud Walsh and flushed several white-tailed deer, an otter, and a bittern. While exploring a tree island called Doctor's Hammock, we saw a swallow-tailed kite and Matthiessen found panther scat. Yesterday evening, as we drove to Monroe Station for dinner, a bobcat sprinted ahead of the car, and last night owls grumbled outside our tent while we used flashlights to read. Such things cause Matthiessen to react as a Wall Street broker might if the Dow suddenly shot up 70 points. "Stick with me," he beamed after seeing the bobcat, "and you'll be farting through silk."

Today, what we will probably be farting through is water. Our plan is to hike from the border of Everglades National Park to a cypress hammock where, in December of 1840, federal troops surprised Chief Chekika and his band. Chekika's group had attacked settlers on Indian Key in the Florida Keys, killing a Dr. Perrine and six others, and to get even, the troops chased Chekika down and hung him from a tree. According to Matthiessen, Florida Indians still refer to the hammock as The Hanging Place, and refuse to go there. As best we can determine, no one else goes there either, which makes it immediately attractive. Before leaving, we stop and talk with Fred Dayhoff, a ranger in the park for many years until a helicopter crash forced his retirement. Dayhoff, who knows the Glades intimately, starts off by calling the swamp ape a bunch of damn nonsense—Dayhoff's forebears were hunters for the railroad, and they would have seen some sign of one, if the creature really existed. Matthiessen listens to this without comment, but says later that the testimony of passionate skeptics has no more credibility than the stories of passionate believers. What Dayhoff does acknowledge is that even Indians shy away from Chekika's Hammock, and that's good enough for us.

O O O

We drive to the border of the national park. Matthiessen must stop twice: once to watch an Everglades kite, then again to inspect the body of an otter that has been killed on the highway. At the park boundary we hike southward along the ridge of a canal for more than a mile, then cut east through a watery prairie. All the way, Matthiessen watches for birds while I, even more intently, keep an eye peeled for water moccasins. There are sedge and cattails, but no saw grass—and no snakes. Chekika's Hammock is a pale-green hedge, two miles away.

It's an easy walk, not nearly so hard as it looked from the road, and we arrive at the northwest tip of the hammock in just under an hour. Matthiessen says he's hot, and suggests we go for a swim in the deeper water that rims the hammock. He points to an area clogged with reeds and fallen limbs—the kind of place where snakes dream of living. This is no surprise to me; Matthiessen's bad about swimming in such places, and I tell him so. He takes this as a veto, and we plunge ahead onto the island, spooking a deer as we go. But here, the going is not so easy. Most tree islands in the Glades are fortresses on the outside but open and cool on the inside, by reason of their own shading. This one is no different, and we have to break our way in, with the webs of golden orb spiders trailing from Matthiessen's head. The low brush thins out into a garden of chest-high ferns, which glow iridescent green in rays of sunlight filtering through the high canopy. There are hardwood trees here—gumbo-limbo, mahogany, and others I don't know. Matthiessen stops abruptly; the silence settles beneath the tittering of birds, and he whispers, "*The Hanging Place.*" For a moment, the island seems alive with its own past, and I would not be surprised to turn and see an echo-image of Chekika's body turning in these wind gusts that violate the stillness from outside. So I do turn—and see what I do not expect to see. Matthiessen sees it too and says aloud, "Aw, crap," for, visible through the trees, is a television antenna.

I push my way through the ferns, and sure enough, it's real: a TV antenna attached to a small green cottage built on a neatly mowed lawn, and a tire swing. A wooden sign over the door reads ELLIS HAMMOCK, and we both hope we are on the wrong island, but then we don't talk about it anymore because we can hear an airboat approaching and, we realize suddenly, we are trespassers—trespassers in a region of Florida where trespassers are not always treated kindly.

Should we run?

No, says Matthiessen, one should never run—a philosophy I don't particularly agree with, but I stand my ground anyway. There is a small lagoon just south of the house, and the sound of the airboat is so loud that it's as if a plane is about to crash. The airboat sweeps around the point of the lagoon toward us, and I wish like hell we had run because I can now see who and what is in the boat. The boat is one of those customized marvels painted fluorescent red with naked women airbrushed on the twin rudders and *Southern Lady* emblazoned on the side. It carries two men and two dogs. The man at the controls wears a short-billed cap and a menacing expression—perhaps he is still angry about losing his right arm. One of the dogs doesn't amount to much, but the other—the beast standing on the bow glaring at us— weighs about 80 pounds and wears a collar of heavy-gauge galvanized chain.

"Christ, it's a pit bull," one of us says, although with all the noise and in such a situation I can't tell if it is Matthiessen's voice or my own. What is clear is that the moment the boat touches land the pit bull is going to lunge ashore and eat one of us—I can tell by the way it is dancing around unrestrained. It is too late to run; there are no trees to climb, and in the few seconds it takes the airboat to cross the last 50 yards of water, my mind works at a furious pace, thrashing out the odds of the dog eating Matthiessen but not me—a lucid interval inspired by a pure love of life. What I know is, Matthiessen has a horror of mean dogs. I once owned such a dog, a Chesapeake Bay retriever named Gator, whom Matthiessen hated as much as the dog hated him. For years he signed his letters, "Kick Gator for me," with a mean-spiritedness that poor Gator badly wanted to repay, but never got the chance. This, I figure, is in my favor—for aren't dogs supposed to sense fear in humans? The trick, I realize, is to make sure the dog senses Matthiessen with his fear before it has an opportunity to sense me with mine.

○ ○ ○

"I think we ought to stand up," I tell Matthiessen, for we are both crouched low—a display of rank submission on my part, but perhaps spiritual for Matthiessen, who is a Zen Buddhist monk. Amazingly, Matthiessen hears me, stands, and takes a step forward. I quickly take two steps back just as the one-armed man skids the airboat onto shore. The pit bull, the biggest pit bull I've seen in my life, bolts immediately for Matthiessen, who yells "whoa!" as if speaking to a horse—a ridiculous finesse that isn't going to work, not if the spirit of my poor dead Gator has anything to do with it. But it does work, and the goddamn dog rushes right past Matthiessen and rams its nose into my crotch.

I whisper, "Nice doggie, nice doggie," standing absolutely frozen.

"This is my camp," calls the one-armed man.

"Right," says Matthiessen. "We hiked in through the back side and didn't realize there was a camp here." He lounges there, smiling like the two of them had just met in some Paris bistro.

My body is stone but my jaw still works. "Sure a good-looking pit bull you got here," I holler. "What's his name?"

The one-armed man yells, "Leave him alone, Buck!" and Buck goes trotting off, staring back as he pisses on bushes, making it clear that he would rather piss on me.

The one-armed man shuts down the engine, and in the sudden quiet it seems that we are all talking too loud. The name of the one-armed man is John Ellis. I never learn the name of the other man, a younger man, for he doesn't say a word the whole time we are there. But once Ellis believes we really didn't come to vandalize his camp, his expression turns from menacing to magnanimous. He wants to show us around and tell us all about the place.

No, we haven't hiked to the wrong island, Ellis says. This is Chekika's Hammock all right, the place where the soldiers hung the Indian

73

way back when. He walks us across the yard to the cottage and explains that the hanging tree stood over there by that wooden porch, but lightning knocked it down—a thing, I can tell, that pleases Matthiessen. It was a big tree, Ellis says, 60 by 60; he measured it. Then he shows us the inside of the cottage, very proud of the job he has done, moving everything—lumber, generator, refrigerator, the whole works—by airboat. Ellis, who lives in Hialeah, says he builds custom airboats, and has been gunkholing around the Glades for 14 years. He isn't put off at all by the fact that our T-shirts say we are looking for swamp apes. In fact, he has a swamp ape story of his own.

"There was a guy at Holiday Park saw one," says Ellis. "Came around the bend in his airboat and saw one climbing a fence. Thought everyone would think he was crazy, but he talked to a highway patrolman and the patrolman said he was *glad* the guy had seen it, 'cause he'd seen the same damn thing a couple of times himself.

"You never know what could be hiding out there," Ellis says. "The Glades is a big place. But, if there really is a swamp ape, I don't think it would hurt you. I stay out here all the time by myself, walk around at night, go out froggin' alone, and I never feel afraid of nothing."

As Matthiessen says after Ellis has given us an airboat ride back to our car, "With that damn dog out there, nothing in its right mind would try to bother him."

Which is exactly the kind of attitude, I tell Matthiessen, that dogs sense, and which probably caused Buck to be friendly to me but ignore him.

○　○　○

It it just after dawn, and we are standing not far from the Shark Valley observation tower, a great cement monolith west of Miami in Everglades National Park and from which people can see miles of saw grass without getting their feet wet. We are about to get our feet very wet, and I am thinking about something else you can see looking down from that tower: alligators. Big ones, too. Hervey Yarbrough, who has replaced Matthiessen on this leg of the expedition, stares at the gators, looks at me, and says, "You're leading the way, right?"

Hervey is a fourth-generation Floridian, and his grandfather, who is still remembered as Big Daddy, was warden at the prison camp on Pine Island. He and I have covered a lot of ground together, and we both rate the same in the courage department. Also with us are three staffers from the North Carolina Outward Bound School (NCOBS): G. Archer Hutchinson (who is Gerald), Nathalie Belanger, and Paul Battle. I stare at the gators, look at Hervey, nod toward the Outward Bounders, and whisper, "Nope. They are."

The Outward Bounders, I figure, will welcome the opportunity, because the NCOBS keeps a permanent base camp in Everglades City, and these three reflect Glades attitudes now long gone: They seek out difficult situations so as to live, during their courses, under the most trying of circumstances—and they do it on purpose.

Our plan is to hike from the observation tower, which is off the Tamiami Trail, through the saw grass of Shark River Slough, to a tidal creek called Rookery Branch, a distance of about 16 miles. Behind us we will pull canoes loaded with gear enough for four days, because once we reach the estuary, we plan to paddle to the Gulf of Mexico, then Flamingo. The route was suggested by an Outward Bound staff member, but the choice of this area—the actual watercourse of the grass river—was inspired by a story I heard from Buddy Roberts, who was born in Flamingo in 1918. Roberts and his family, along with many other Glades settlers, were chased out of their homes when the National Park Service took over in 1947, and he's still angry about it. Roberts told me that a hunting buddy of his had seen—and he had heard—a swamp ape several miles southwest of Shark Valley. Thinking of that sound, that high-pitched wail, the friend said, still made his hair stand up. But Roberts said he didn't really believe it was a swamp ape. Nope. His buddy had been drinking, he explained, and such creatures just don't exist.

The problem is, no one hikes through Shark Valley—that's what the woman on the phone at Everglades National Park told me. For one thing, the country's too rough, and for another, it's just not allowed. But then I spoke with Mike Finley, superintendent of Everglades National Park. He had never heard of the swamp ape, but sure, we could have permission to go look for it. He even wanted to go with us, but couldn't.

The previous night, staying at the NCOBS base camp in Everglades City, I had received an omen as to just how lucky Finley was to stay behind. Back in the brush, as I was cutting hiking staves with a knife that was more like a machete, Hervey had said, "Watch you don't stick that thing into your leg," which I proceeded to do on the next swing. Hervey thought this was pretty funny, having warned me and all, and I was chuckling, too—until I got a look at the cut under the light. We couldn't get the bleeding stopped, and it never really did stop for four days. But we couldn't let the Outward Bounders know. As gung ho as they are in some respects, they're finicky about safety and, presumably, about the competence of people with whom they travel.

The Outward Bounders are loading the canoes cheerfully, moving around in the fresh morning light, smiling like they're with someone who knows what he's doing. Mike Finley is here to see us off, but isn't smiling because he is telling me about an Air Force proposal to establish a Military Operations Area directly over Everglades National Park. If the proposal is approved by the FAA, he says, F-16 and F-4 fighters will do intercept-training over the Glades at an altitude as low as 100 feet, and at speeds in excess of 400 mph. "In my opinion," he says, "it's like sponsoring a Roller Derby in the Sistine Chapel. The proposal shows a real lack of sensitivity on the part of the Air Force, and a degree of arrogance."

I give Finley a swamp ape T-shirt before we take a last look at the observation tower and shove off.

○ ○ ○

Pulling a canoe through heavy saw grass and knee-deep water, I soon discover, is not a speed sport. Forty minutes after starting, we are just abreast of the tower, having covered about a half-mile.

I glance at Hervey, who already looks tired, and tell him, "It's bound to get easier." After my walk with Matthiessen, I am convinced that it is so. But there was no saw grass on the way to Chekika's Hammock. And I am wrong about it getting easier.

I once jogged the Orange Bowl Marathon and, after 18 miles, tried to flag down a bus because I thought I was exhausted. I wasn't exhausted. I don't think I was ever exhausted in my life until Shark Valley. Here's the way it is pulling a canoe through saw grass: You take one step, sink to your thigh in muck and periphyton algae, then with the next step kick sharp limestone rock known as Miami oolite. Every yard is an adventure because you're walking in water and can't see what awaits beneath. The canoes, loaded with gear, should float, but they don't. The saw grass clings to the aluminum, making a sound like fingernails on a chalkboard as we muscle onward. We have made rope harnesses, and, tied to the canoes, one person pulls while another pushes. There is no shade; the saw grass and sun are old allies; the earth is saturated with heat.

This isn't a hike, it's an endurance trial, and coming here under the guise of looking for a swamp ape now seems worse than ridiculous, it seems stupid. The Indians who lived here had a word for the creature, which may have translated as "the sand person," so sightings in the area probably predate the twentieth century. Yet these facts do nothing to dent the reality of fighting one's way step by step though the saw grass.

I keep hoping, keep waiting, for the trail to broaden, to get easier, for we are on a trail of sorts: an airboat path that rangers travel in wetter seasons to check hydrological stations. The grass, often higher than our heads, has been fanned apart as if touched by mad dust devils, but the going is still agonizingly slow, a mile an hour at best. In 1838 a surgeon serving with the U.S. Army in the Seminole War described traveling the Glades as "intolerable. . .excruciating," and he was describing going over an oolite flat, not through swamp. We are in swamp, with water up to our chests in one place, not high enough to float the canoes in another.

Still behind us is the Shark Valley observation tower. In just three hours I have come to despise the look of it. Tourists watch us through binoculars; they must think us crazy. We pull for another hour, and the tower still looms, as if it has somehow been tethered to the canoes and we are pulling it with us.

Maybe the tourists are right.

As we pull, seven glossy ibis bank over us in loose formation, their wings making a dry whistle in the heat. Then a marsh hawk lands in a stunted myrtle bush, carrying a writhing snake. Seeing these things is as refreshing as the water we gulp. When we do talk, it's not about the swamp ape. The Outward Bounders are open to the possibility of its existence, but any hopes of seeing such a thing have been replaced by the more pragmatic hope that the hiking will get easier. Mostly we just concentrate on pulling and breathing.

I like these people I am with. Paul and Nathalie are both French-Canadian, although only Nathalie has an accent. Nathalie also has blonde hair, is very pretty, and belches often and without reserve—a practice she says still troubles her mother. Paul has a beard and an earring, and Gerald was born in Rockingham, North Carolina, my maternal home and where most of the Baptist churches have deacons who are my uncles. I'm already tired, but at ease. These people are livable and among the best at what they do.

Three miles out, we break for lunch, laughing among ourselves. Gerald says he hasn't eaten white bread in years; Nathalie belches, while Paul puzzles over a way to make the pulling harnesses more effective. Without Hervey and me, the Outward Bounders would have been able to go faster, but they don't seem to mind. They're in good spirits. We're moving slowly, but we're still moving, and the farther we go, the deeper the water should get—that's what I have been told, anyway. Soon we'll be able to do some paddling, thank God. After only four hours, I'm exhausted. Maybe Hervey is, too. But we're going to make it.

Hervey and I sit side by side on a canoe, eating. He and I have traveled all of Florida, some of the United States, Central America, and the Caymans, and spent ten days in Mariel Harbor, Cuba, awaiting refugees during the boat lift. He looks up from his sandwich, grins, and says, "One day I'm going to follow you right off the edge of the damn earth."

At this pace and in this heat, I think, the edge might not be far away. I suggest that we begin to monitor our own pulse rates—this is no place to deal with heat exhaustion or a heart attack. Hervey's expression tells me he thinks I'm taking safety a little too far. In truth I'm just plain scared by a discovery I have made in the last four hours: One does not travel the Glades; one is trapped by it in varying degrees of time and distance until one is free entirely. Out here, a serious health problem would be fatal.

I spend the remaining rest period thinking about the people who found escape in this saw grass; about how desperate, how utterly desperate, the Indians must have been to come here. Before me, the grass fans to the horizon, a plain of light and space broken only by the domes of tree islands where the Indians once hid. Now, it seems to me, the silence of those islands vibrates with all the terror that has ever been or ever will be, because I know now, as only one who has hiked the saw grass can know, that nothing but terror could drive a people into the heart of this land. From the safety of a park boardwalk, the Everglades may be a cerebral delight, but when one is exhausted and on foot, mired in the bowels of it, the Glades rings with a visceral horror implied by its own history. I smile, joke with the others, and point out a cluster of apple snail eggs growing on a stalk of saw grass. But being here is not fun; it is frightening.

The wind stirs and the saw grass trembles in random patterns as a cloud crosses the sun. The cloud's shadow, big as a ship, drifts past us in graduated shades of gray, then gold, gaining speed as the light freshens.

Tying himself to a canoe, Gerald says, "If the swamp ape doesn't live around here, it should. No rational person would look for it here."

Nathalie nods her head up and down emphatically.

Hervey says, "You know, a beer would be good right now."

Nathalie nods her head once more.

We begin to pull again.

We pull, step by brutalizing step, for five more hours. My muscles cramp, my lungs burn, my head pounds from heat and oxygen debt, and still we press on, until finally the observation tower has been dwarfed by our efforts.

But something is wrong. Instead of the water gradually getting deeper, it has gotten shallower, until now there is none. For the last mile we have been muscling the boats through clay mud and thick grass, expecting to find water, but it never materializes. This can't go on much longer, and an hour before sunset, we stop to reconnoiter ahead.

Gerald and I walk on for more than a mile, and still no water. We walk farther yet, but without finding even the two inches it would take to float our packed canoes.

We had figured that we had about 16 miles of saw grass to cross before reaching the tidal creeks of Whitewater Bay. Now, after covering nearly half the distance, *this*. If we could somehow abandon the canoes, we could make it. Or, if we could find water, we could make it because going forward could in no way be more difficult than going back. Whatever the situation, the Outward Bounders, if on their own, probably would have pushed ahead; worked out a portage system, or cut cross-country. But, with this unexpected absence of water, we begin to wonder if we haven't come too far west, or maybe followed a wrong trail. Everything looks the same, and all we have are compasses and the newest of charts—which means the charts were made decades ago.

The Swamp Ape

As it turned out, we had neither gone too far west nor followed a wrong trail. All we had run into was Rattlesnake Ridge, and with loaded canoes, there was no hope of making it from the start.

○ ○ ○

That night, Miami, far to the east, permeates the sky, glowing with the same bleak fluorescence as a bus station. We lie on the canoes, concentrating on the sky above, listening to the cries of night birds. More tired than I have ever been in my life, more tired than I thought I could ever be, I rest here feeling the thud of my own heart, wondering if it might not quit rather than try the trip back again. I despise the thought of it, of seeing that damn observation tower once more, so I listen, instead, to the Outward Bounders, as they try to buoy my spirits. They remind me of the birds we have seen; of the four deer we flushed so close we could hear the rasp of their breathing. But no swamp ape—this said with gentle laughter, although they know I do not believe.

Twenty hours later, with one shoe sole missing, limping badly, cut and cramped all to hell, I flag down a Shark Valley tram driven by Tony Espejo. Espejo is halfway through his tour, but he is kind enough to stop anyway. His is the last tram of the day, and he offers to take me to Shark Valley headquarters where I can phone for transport for the canoes, which now rest on the bank near the observation tower after a nine-hour hike that was even more miserable than that of the previous day.

There is only one seat available on the bus, the one beside Tony, and it faces 42 camera-carrying tourists who are as startled to look up and see me as I am to see them. They smell of suntan lotion and shampoo; I smell and look like a zoo exhibit. There is a lot of silence; I expect to hear the click of shutters, capturing this aberration right along with the lethargic gators and wading birds. Instead, a nice woman in a dress pipes up: "Were you really out hiking in the saw grass?" and I realize that she has read my T-shirt.

Yes, I tell her, we were really out there.

What's it like? she wants to know, and everyone on the bus is listening.

I tell her the truth. I tell her not to try it, not even to think about it, and I mean what I say, every word. Because, as the Seminoles and the soldiers who chased them discovered, and as people who settled on the fringe of the saw grass must have surely known, there is a creature out there—one that can't be seen from a boardwalk or described in a book; a creature that does not walk on two legs, but endures.

They Shall Inherit

Houston? Apollo eleven. I've got the world in my window . . .

—ASTRONAUT MICHAEL COLLINS,
18 July 1969

There's a moon tonight so, viewed from within, my dome tent glows like those attractive tent advertisements favored by catalog companies: a luminous capsule containing the silhouette of a solitary traveler.

The traveler's aspect, at least, is sensual; mine is only sweaty.

Friends and I are camped on a spoil island in Mosquito Lagoon, an estuary that is part of Canaveral National Seashore and Merritt Island National Wildlife Refuge. Around most of America, the weather is autumnal, but on the east coast of Florida even the moon seems to radiate heat. Yet I wear long pants and boots because of the bugs. Most Floridians consider it lunacy to camp before December, but we have paddled sea kayaks to this island to view an extraordinary event from a vantage point few people realize is available and even fewer access.

Through my screened tent flap, I can see twin obelisks created by a lighted scaffolding 12 miles away: Kennedy Space Center's Complex 39, where the space shuttle *Columbia,* on a pad 400-feet tall, stands ready to launch.

Or so we hope.

With more than an hour before scheduled lift-off, however, I am not looking at the shuttle pad. I am watching large insects chart their way across the iridescent skin of my tent. When I first noticed them, there were three, then eight, now more than a dozen, waving their antennae experimentally before each short ascent, testing the screened windows, examining each seam.

I reach up, rap the roof, and the insects scatter in a frenzy, only to regroup and begin their slow exploration once more.

They are cockroaches. Great big cockroaches, all the color of demon nicotine. Roaches are everywhere on this unnamed island; they own the damn place, yet it seems they won't be content until they conquer my tent as well.

Clearly, they don't know that a natural enemy lies within. Me, the natural enemy.

○ ○ ○

We left early this morning from LeFlis Fish Camp, a Florida anachronism with its old fish house and reeling docks, paddling ten miles through another east coast rarity: wild shoreline with a horizon unbroken by the stalagmite crust of hotels. This preserve, established because the Space Center required a security buffer, is the only continuous undeveloped piece of coast between Jacksonville and Miami, 700 miles, and abandoning my car for a boat was like being able to breathe again. Canaveral National Seashore is a window not entirely dissimilar from the one through which Michael Collins once gazed. It is a lone portal onto a miniaturized world.

They Shall Inherit

I am here at the invitation of Larry Willis of Southern Exposure Sea Kayaks who, months earlier, had described to me his plan to paddle as close to Cape Canaveral as the law allowed, then watch a night launch from camp on some small island.

"The night of a launch," Willis had told me, "the roads, the hotels are jammed with tourists. But get out there in Mosquito Lagoon, and there's almost no one. We can get a lot closer that way, too."

Now, after many delays—the Space Center's, and my own—I have finally rendezvoused with Willis and seven of his paddling friends, finding them expert kayakers and comfortable companions, all willing to endure the heat, the bugs, and a novice paddler (me) for the chance of a clear view of the shuttle. But early this morning, each of us heard radio reports that NASA had discovered new problems with *Columbia*. One of us says the problem is a broken telephone on the launch pad, another says they are putting in a new fuel pump. Once on the water, we will have no access to updates, but we leave anyway, telling each other these are minor problems and will certainly be fixed in time for the launch at 1:30 a.m.

Now it is after midnight, and I lie in the heat with a clear view of the shuttle pad, but I can't seem to take my eyes off these roaches. I know they are only insects, one tough link in a magnificent chain, but I have a near-organic prejudice that defines them differently: winged maggots with the speed of rats. I wonder if this island has the largest population I have ever seen: certainly it does. But then I remember a time years ago, dreaming that something was climbing on my body, over my hands, my legs, crawling across my face—then waking up in the Third World squalor of a slum apartment to find I was not dreaming.

The time for the launch comes and goes. Yet another hour passes. I can hear the distant barrage of surf on the beach and, with each variation in pitch, I tell myself it is the roar of engines firing. It is not. Finally, I lunge out of the tent, zip it quickly behind me, then walk to the shore and stare across the bay at Cape Canaveral. There has been so much international attention focused on this wide strip of beach that

85

one might expect it to be slightly scorched; cratered by the collective mind waves of the world. Instead, I see a charcoal hedge of mangroves, the stolid glow of the shuttle lights, and I feel again a wave of emotion, like seeing the Lincoln Memorial for the first time. The fact that NASA has fallen on hard times in recent years doesn't matter. It doesn't matter that employees are complaining that the 30-year-old buildings are moldy, falling apart, and that they have to put garbage cans beneath the leaks when it rains. And it doesn't matter that the Hubble space telescope is failing, or that NASA has been trying to get *Columbia* off the ground since May, because I can see it, right over there, and from that spot men left for the *moon,* for God's sake.

Perhaps *Columbia* isn't going to fly this night, either, and my private suspicion is that a roach has scampered up a cable or something; maybe gnawed through one of the bulkheads to get high on hydrogen. I suffer a brief mental image of a NASA technician fighting off cockroaches with one hand while straining toward the moon with the other. No outrage is beyond these six-legged bastards, and that they triumph so effortlessly whispers an irony far more subtle than the noise of my boots clomping back to the tent, twin assassins on a mission a quarter of a million years old.

○ ○ ○

A quarter of a million years is how long we've been trying to kill them, but roaches have been around for much longer. They were already a terrestrial success story when dinosaurs emerged, and roaches probably fed on the last dinosaur corpse a hundred million years later. Roaches are older than the Alps, older than Pikes Peak, older than the North Pole ice cap. Roach fossils have been found in rocks dating back 280 million years, and they will probably be found fossilized in rocks 280 million years from today—if there is anyone around to find them.

Or so suggested Dr. David A. Nickle, a research entomologist with the Smithsonian Institution, whom I recently called to ask for help in identifying the species that held dominion on that small island—the great big black variety that makes a cheery popping sound beneath one's boots. Dr. Nickle told me it was probably the Florida woods roach, though he was reluctant to say for certain without seeing it. Then, perceiving my distaste for the creatures, he also suggested that my dislike was irrational.

"Cockroaches are actually very gentle animals," he told me. "Of the 3,500 or so species on earth, only about 50 species are found in the United States. And, of those 50, only about eight are domestic or para-domestic."

This is supposed to be good news for those of us who prefer the outdoors?

Well, their life history is interesting too, Nickle said, and suggested I do some reading. I did. Some species of cockroaches have scent glands that produce a bitter almond-scented liquid, which allows them to leave a trail of inky spittle so they can find their way at night. Prior to mating, the female drags its vibrating wings along the ground while the male scampers backward and rams his genitalia in. They may remain in that position for up to 24 hours. Some species of female cockroaches need mate only once to produce young the remainder of their lives, which is why male roaches are attracted only to virgins. Their blood has a lower freezing point than water, they can survive on far less oxygen than man, they can evolve resistance to specific insecticides within three or four generations, and there are strains of cockroaches, in fact, that appear to have evolved resistance to *all* insecticides.

"But they are a valid life form," Dr. Nickle told me. "They're not dirty in the way that rats are dirty, and it's interesting to note that their nearest relative, the praying mantis, is revered around the world, yet it is far more voracious. Cockroaches do a lot of good. They're part of the detritus breakdown. They eat leaves and rotting litter and convert it to simpler substances. Frankly, they do a lot more good than man, in my opinion."

But then I spoke with Dr. Philip Koehler, professor at the University of Florida and an urban entomologist, who has spent the last 20 years researching how to control roaches. His view of the animal was not so rosy.

"More than 50 different kinds of disease organisms have been found in cockroaches or their excrement," he said, "including polio and hepatitis. But because they're often the same kind of diseases that can be passed by a dirty hand, it's very difficult to prove roaches spread disease. But they undoubtedly have in the past.

"One of the problems," he said, "is that they're so prolific. They thrive in disturbed urban habitat. A few years ago, we did a count in low-income housing and found an average of 1,500 roaches per apartment. We did a similar count in an outdoor area near Tampa and found an average of a quarter of a million cockroaches per acre. In other words, if you see one, there're usually a lot more. What makes it even more challenging is that, for every technological advance we are able to make in the area of controlling cockroaches, they quickly evolve ways to overcome those techniques."

Both researchers agree that the insect is a genetic marvel. As Dr. Nickle told me, "Cockroaches will undoubtedly outlast man as a group."

○ ○ ○

At 4 a.m., I am still awake, though I am convinced now that the shuttle will not be launched. Later, I will learn that a fuel leak has caused the mission to be scrubbed—for the third time in four months. The Associated Press will describe the postponement as "the latest blow to NASA's image," though such safety precautions might be more correctly viewed as a moral triumph.

Actually, I don't mind that *Columbia* didn't fly. Just so long as I can take a good long swim when the sun gets up . . . and have some of

Larry Willis's fried fish ... then maybe learn how to roll a kayak. A hot tent inspires a wistfulness more practical than visionary, and now, lying in the heat, looking out through my own small window to the world, only the basics matter. I can see the moon; its craters form a human face. I can see the lights of the broken shuttle. And I could reach out and touch those dark creatures waiting at the screen.

Hanoi Jane Goes to
Shooting School

*J*ane and Ted are supposed to be around here somewhere.

"Somewhere" is Jefferson County, north Florida, which is oak hammock and quail shooting country. "Here" is the Orvis Shooting School at Mays Pond Plantation, a 4,500-acre preserve where monied sportsmen from across the country fly in to hone their wing-shooting skills. The nearest town is Monticello, population 5,000, and there was an article in today's Monticello paper that said Jane had stopped by Gelling's Florists to order flowers. I find the article interesting because it lends credence to the rumor that she and Ted are here to attend the Orvis school in preparation for a quail hunt on Ted's South Carolina plantation.

For a place the size of Monticello, Jane's arrival is exciting news. But for one who has signed up for the school (I have), the news is confounding too.

It is easy enough to imagine Jane strolling down the shaded streets of Monticello and popping into Gelling's to inspect the gladiolus and bachelor's buttons. Perhaps she wore the *Electric Horseman* ensemble: suede boots, designer jeans, and a purse not much bigger than a Gold Card. The difficulty is in trying to transfer this image to a field of Carolina silage where she will shoulder a 20-gauge Beretta and blast small birds from the sky.

Ted? Sure, no problem picturing Ted. Ted will tamp in a pinch of snuff, call the dogs, piss on the fire, and have the cook gutting his kill before Bernard Shaw does the CNN world round-up.

But Jane?

There is an odd dynamic at work here; a compromise of boundaries that, for some, must be unsettling. For people who see these two as symbols, it could say something about the dilution of ideals or illustrate, perhaps, the mind-set of this new decade, the Melded Age. Even for those of us who don't much care, the union goads a reinspection of the perimeters of outdoor sports.

Had Linnaeus grouped them, there would be two broad families of outdoor disciplines. There would be the harmony sports, such as camping, skiing, kayaking, hiking, climbing, biking, sailing, orienteering, bird-watching, and probably nude sunbathing too. And there would be the dissonant sports, which might include snowmobiling, four-wheeling, three-wheeling, jet skiing, trapping, cattle rustling, bait fishing, spearfishing, motorboating, arson—and, of course, hunting.

There are probably a few crossover sports too, such as fly-fishing and mountain biking. Maybe even skeet shooting, if you want to stretch it.

Otherwise, the poles and the politics are sharply defined. If you are a purist, you probably embrace only one family and look upon the other as bastard offspring. Personally, economic necessity has mongrelized my ideals. A lack of virtue has probably played a part too. I enjoy most of the one and a little bit of the other.

But Jane?

Hanoi Jane Goes to Shooting School

O O O

Norm says, "Jane? The last time she had a gun in her hand was probably Hanoi."

Norm and Ed and I are the only ones who have shown up on this first crisp morning of the Orvis Shooting School. In the forest around us, leaves have turned, so the dominant colors are yellow and rust. Down by the pond, smoke drifts from the chimney of the one-room cabin where our instructors, Darring and Rick, gave a safety orientation and showed us a short video on the Churchill method of wing-shooting, the English technique favored by Orvis.

The instructors also told us that "a couple of other" students might arrive later in the day, or even tomorrow.

Now Ed and Norm and I, strangers until this morning, are off by ourselves for the first time, standing at the beginner's trap (a device that flings disks called "sporting clays") waiting for Darring to bring ammunition. Our conversation is relaxed, mildly exploratory, seeking common ground. They have heard the rumors too.

Ed considers Norm's remark about Hanoi and says, "I doubt if she could hit something that didn't have an American flag on it."

To which I add, "Just as long as we don't have to stop and do aerobics," which is suggestive enough to cement the alliance—an alliance I am happy to join, by the way. For one thing, they are not talking about Jane the person—the woman who stepped into Gelling's and ordered flowers. Their jokes concern ideals contrary to their own, and I think they have couched their positions with just the right flavor of tolerance. The tolerance is in their tone, of course—the punch lines spoken wryly, with the bitterness leached away by two decades. And, if the tables were turned, I suspect Ed and Norm, with their thousand-dollar shotguns and four-wheel-drive vehicles, would be portrayed with far more bitterness if described in the lexicon of Hollywood or Fifth Avenue. And just as unfairly.

Batfishing in the Rainforest

Recently, I read an article in *Esquire* magazine about Ed and Norm (not actually about these two, but about the Eds and Norms across the land, the American hunter) in which the author banged her fist and railed at the injustice of these potbellied men who used expensive phallic symbols to terrorize and maim all creatures great and small. The author was so convinced of her virtuous stand that the story had no credibility. Even her own lean facts wilted in the heat of her bias.

I agreed with almost nothing in the piece. But the author had conviction; she had the fire of her ideals, and she wielded them without apology—an uncommon thing in this decade of the soft voice; a decade in which a new-age sensitivity has pinned a lot of heads to the floor. The new-age rules are unspoken, but the rules are there. You don't use words that might cause offense. You don't take controversial stands unless that controversy has been validated by new-age standards. You don't libel—you seek a rational compromise.

This is the quiet time, and the stink of bureaucratic caution seeps from all quarters. One keeps one's nose down and stays in line. This is the time of the great blending.

So I liked the *Esquire* story, though I was not swayed. I would have enjoyed it even more if the author had not attacked one of the few groups that the shield of new-age sensitivity has yet to protect. But the woman let it hang out, by God. She shot from the hip. She jumped up on the turret and told her truth.

Jane and Ted could show up at any moment. But there's no chance the author of that *Esquire* story will be among the new arrivals coming to sharpen their skills for blood sport.

In these strange times, though, who can be sure? Whether this is the Melded Age or the Gelded Age depends on which end of the barrel you stare down.

○ ○ ○

I enjoy hunting. It's the killing I don't like. So I don't—kill, I mean. Oh, I eat the things that have been killed for me, pigs and cows and asparagus stems, but I shy away from doing it myself. I am comfortable with the hypocrisy, unless I have to argue the position. So I don't do that either—argue, I mean.

In my preteens, I used to hunt and kill. I ran a trap line too. Before school, on alternate mornings, I would walk the trap line and gather the drowned muskrats, which I then sold in town. One morning, though, I rounded the bend to find a skunk that had not drowned. The skunk turned its butt to me in defiance, then almost immediately collapsed on its belly, exhausted from fighting against the trap, which had shattered its leg. The animal had been in the trap for, what, a few hours? Maybe all night. Maybe all day and all night. It lay there panting, head still but eyes moving with every move I made. In that animal I perceived all the horrors then known to me: bloody disfigurement, physical suffering and terror, plus a new one—the stricken look of complete submission. That look, a kind of endorphin numbness, was the most disturbing thing I had ever seen. That look was death; not the silence that followed it. In a panic, I shot the skunk with my shotgun, and the creature wilted before my eyes. Its head smoldered, like a flame gone out.

Since that day, I have killed only one other thing with a gun, and that was a duck for a retriever who I felt deserved the opportunity to ply its trade. I still accompany people who hunt because I like the way it feels and smells. On those rare occasions when I do carry a gun, I shoot to miss, thus establishing, among my hunting friends, the fiction that I am an extraordinarily bad shot.

At least I thought it was a fiction.

After my first day here at the Orvis Shooting School, I am not so sure. Norm and Ed and I have each paid $725 for this course, for which we are to receive instruction, a fitting for a custom-built Orvis shotgun (should we decide to buy one), a diploma suitable for framing, and, according to Darring's promise, "The chance to shoot more in two days than you've ever shot before. Probably five or six hundred rounds."

Darring was not exaggerating.

We shoot and shoot and shoot, then move to a new trap station and shoot some more. Darring loads our guns a shot at a time, then he springs the trap. Norm and Ed and I take turns trying to blast the clay bird. After most shots, Darring or Rick offers warm advice or warmer compliments. They are good at what they do.

But shooting clay targets is not as easy as it looks. The school has loaned me a Beretta 20-gauge; a beautiful over-and-under that I handle gingerly because the replacement cost, according to the catalog, is $2,500. At some stations, it seems this gun can't miss. At others, I begin to wonder if pellets are really coming out of the barrel.

Once I complain to Darring, "Crap, I couldn't hit a hockey goalie if he was handcuffed to a tree."

"But your form is good," he reassures. "The muscle memory is beginning to show."

As in climbing and kayaking, and maybe even in four-wheeling, too, good shooting is a discipline through which one imprints one's personal sense of order upon the wild. The Churchill method of wing-shooting requires good form, so I am pleased by Darring's compliment.

As Ed points out, the clay targets break anyway once they hit the ground.

○ ○ ○

Rick tells us, "Jane left the day before you guys arrived. She didn't want to shoot with a group, plus she was scheduled to hunt with Ted yesterday." Rick does not say this as an announcement; it's just something that comes out in conversation this morning of the second day.

So Jane was already cracking birds while we were here practicing our gun mounts and follow-through. One of us says, "I wonder if she wore gloves so she wouldn't get blood on her hands."

Then Rick explains the mystery of the late arrivals when he tells Darring, "We're not going to get any more people for this class. Governor Chiles's office just called. He and Sam Nunn are going to quail hunt in Georgia, so they'll reschedule the school later."

Sam Nunn is Sam Nunn, and Lawton Chiles is the Democratic governor of Florida. My old trapper instincts stir. This section of woods called Mays Pond Plantation seems to be a crossing path for power brokers. Sam and Lawton, Ted and Jane, and God knows who else has met or will meet in this private place.

"Good thing they didn't show," Ed says to me. "With Lawton and Jane both here, I wouldn't trust myself with a gun in my hands." He smiles. "Or trust them with a gun in theirs."

Not that we are more than mildly interested. No. Ed and Norm and I have been too focused on trying to break these damn clay birds. The Florida duck season will open soon, and both Ed and Norm are trying to ferret out old flaws in their gunning techniques before going to the blinds.

As Norm says, "I've just never been a very good shot, and I don't know why."

Darring and Rick have discovered why. Norm shoots right-handed, but his left eye is his dominant eye. Same with Ed. The instructors have placed a tiny piece of tape on the left lens of each man's shooting glasses and, *voilà,* both men are suddenly lethal wing-shooters.

"The ducks," beams Norm, "might actually have something to fear, for once."

The ducks have nothing to fear from me. What I want to take away from this two-day Orvis course is the formal knowledge of an exacting sport. My oldest son, age ten, is suddenly hot to hunt, and I want the information I pass on to him to be sound. He will be shooting the same shotgun I used when I was his age, the 410-gauge Mossberg I baled hay to buy and that he has spent his evenings cleaning and oiling.

If my son pulls the trigger and is not stricken by the dark thing that stares back at him, then that is fine. If he pulls the trigger and smells the smoldering flame, that is fine too. He wants to hunt, so I will take him. I will take him because I want him to hear the shrill voices, not just the muted chorus of this nervous decade. I want his head up so the voices can find him: the just, the zealots, the racists, the wise, the rational, the drunks and sons-of-bitches, the weak, the militant, and the haughty rich too. I want my son to climb his own turret and see his own bright truth. And the union of new-age power brokers be damned.

There is too much blood on the ground for it to be otherwise, and not just in the quail fields of South Carolina.

ON THE
WATER

How to Be a Competent
Southern Waterperson

here are probably more than ten things you should know to be considered a Competent Southern Waterperson (CSW), but there are at least ten things you *must* know if you care anything at all about not embarrassing yourself or us (meaning your fellow CSWs). I should say right off that these ten things have nothing at all to do with the Ten rules of Water Safety or the Ten Things to Remember at the Beach. You often read those sort of rules in stories that say things like, "Make sure you pack plenty of sunscreen." That advice is sound enough, but it's a little too obvious for a professional charter boat captain such as me, which is why I never read it. Because of this, I can't guarantee I haven't included a few crossover rules, but it's real unlikely.

1 Don't go where you see birds standing: This rule has to do with boating in shallow water. There's a lot of it in the South—shallow water, I mean—and you need to learn how to deal with it. Here's a tip:

When you're in unfamiliar, unmarked shoal-type areas, look for those long, slick streaks you've probably noticed but never thought much about. Those slicks are usually created by the oily exhaust of a boat that passed before you, and could mark a safe route. Now here's the crucial part: If you do run aground, for God's sake, act like you *meant* to do it. This is especially true if there are other boaters around to gawk and laugh. The moment you feel that sickening thud of hull and prop hitting bottom, shut off the engine. This is not only better for the engine, it underlines the impression that you wouldn't be sitting high and dry if you damn well didn't choose to be there. Then calmly step out into the water and pretend you're looking for something—something *important*. Hand gestures are good here; carrying a sack that could hold a lot of money is better. If you're really convincing you might lure other boaters onto the shoal, which will almost certainly take the focus of attention off you. But even if you're no actor, you can still push your boat off the shoal with a sense of dignity. And getting out of an embarrassing spot with dignity is much of what being a CSW is about.

2 If it works, don't fix it: This concerns boat maintenance and the irrational urge we get to tighten squeaky bolts or tamper with other innocent engine parts that are working just fine but will almost certainly break the moment we lay our hands on them. This wouldn't be so bad, but, on a boat, one small catastrophe always leads to another. So if that bolt you're tightening breaks off—and you don't stop right then and there—you can almost bet you'll end up having to replace the whole engine.

3 Always use a bucket: This rule has to do with voiding, a biological function that makes no concessions to time or place, such as being on a small boat in broad daylight. Did you know that a high percentage of boating fatalities are directly linked to unsafe voiding? We're not talking about kidney damage here. We're talking about boaters concentrating on one thing when they should be concentrating on two things, which is why they fall overboard, get clunked on the head by the hull, and then are chopped up by the prop or die unexpectedly while trying to breathe water. It's no joke: Many unwary voiders are seriously injured or killed every year. So you should always use a bucket or a can. And the boat should be stopped. Since I normally deal with strangers on my 20-foot charter boat—and often female strangers—voiding can be exceedingly awkward, which is why I play music. I hand them the bucket, shove in the cassette tape, and then those of us not involved pretend to look at that pelican way, way over there. For men, I favor Waylon Jennings or Willie Nelson; women usually get Dvořák—all the timpani and strings add a ceremonious flair they seem to appreciate. Before I installed my tape deck, I used to just keep the engine running. But that's not a good idea. Several years ago, with a family of four on board, I was voiding off the stern with the engine running when the youngest son punched the boat into gear. I tumbled off into the water while the mother and father, in a panic, tried to figure out how to stop my boat. I chased the boat, then the boat chased me. That's how I became a strong advocate of buckets. It also brings us to rule number four.

4 Teach someone else how to run the boat: I know this sounds like a prissy rule, but wouldn't you feel a little put out if, right in the middle of your first heart attack, you had to explain to your companion the nuances of throttle or trim? Or say you'd tumbled off the stern while voiding—same deal. It's a good idea to plan for those times when you just don't want to be bothered.

5 Don't lose your head over a hat: Though it sounds trivial, this is another leading cause of boating fatalities: A hat flies off while you're under way, the skipper turns back to get it, someone reaches to grab the hat, falls overboard, and the boat runs over him, ruining a perfectly good hat and probably a perfectly good person. In more than

2,000 charters, I have watched hundreds of hats fly overboard, but I have lost only two hats and no people, so I feel qualified to give some advice here. As you turn back for the hat, designate who you want to pick it up. Human nature being what it is, everyone aboard will lunge for the hat unless you make your wishes clear. Ideally, your hat grabber should be equipped with a landing net. Idle directly toward the hat, then, at the last moment, turn the wheel away from the side of the boat on which your hat grabber is standing and put the engine in neutral. This way, the boat will slide right into the hat and, if your hat grabber falls overboard, an engaged propeller will not disengage him from some useful appendage. There are some exceptions to this rule: If the hat says "I Love New Jersey" or "Go Buckeyes," then, with a completely clear conscience, you may tell everyone aboard to stay seated while you accelerate over it.

6 Don't make an ass of yourself while docking: This rule is designed to elevate you above that unsavory cast of nimrods and coneheads who come charging into docks completely disorganized, the husband yelling at the wife about what lines to grab, the wife screaming at the husband about slowing down, while their vessel plays pinball with any boat or piling that happens to be handy. I don't want to be unkind, but, frankly, I feel people like this should either be sterilized or banished to the promised land. They play no viable role in the South's maritime future, and their peculiar genetic lineage should be interrupted. If you are the skipper of a boat and you feel you need help docking, tell your people exactly what you want them to do long before you get to the dock. If you have to raise your voice for any reason, either you have not done your job, or you are dealing with nimrods and coneheads, in which case reread this paragraph and take the appropriate steps.

7 Those also serve who just sit there like a bump: This relates to rule number five, but it's directed at do-gooders and other troublemakers who sometimes disguise themselves as passengers. If I had the nerve, I'd have two signs posted on my boat: "Don't, Under Any Circumstances, Try to Help," and "All Walleye Stories and Other Ridiculous Lies Forbidden." (For more about walleye stories and how to lie, see rule number ten.) I'm talking about those people who rush, uninvited, to drop your anchor (they almost always throw it), pull up your anchor (then leave your anchor line in a tangled mess), or lunge to fend you off a dock when you don't need fending, thereby knocking you into another boat. They're quick to tie lines to cleats, too—using rat-size knots that can't be untied and have to be cut. These people might do fine in government service where such perverse non-help is expected, but they're a real pain on the water. As a passenger who aspires to be a CSW, you need to learn how to coil a rope. You need to remember that anchor dropping is not an Olympic event, and you need to learn to tie at least one knot—a half hitch, though if you can also learn a clove hitch and a bowline, so much the better. But, mostly, you need to learn how to just sit there.

8 Only two kinds of people buy boats—fools and us: This rule is included to separate the Competent Southern Waterperson from other normally intelligent, well-adjusted people who—suffering some momentary lapse of sanity, perhaps—go ahead and buy a boat anyway. We rationalize what should otherwise be an embarrassment by pretending to anticipate what other boat buyers don't: that we'll spend about twice as much money on fuel, storage, and maintenance as we'd planned, while having about a third as much fun as we'd hoped.

9 Don't do dumb things: This is a much-needed miscellaneous category, kind of like, "Go, and sin no more" in the Bible. You're not always going to be on a boat, so it's good to remember that you can make a fool of yourself in other places too, such as at the beach. A nice husband and wife once chartered my boat and, on the way to a deserted island, the man whispered that he wanted me to drop them off on the beach and then disappear for two hours. The wife may have planned on looking for seashells, but the husband obviously had romance on his mind. I left them on the beach and, when I returned two hours later, they were both standing in water up to their shoulders. The husband looked troubled, and the woman's face was red (and, I should stress, this was a *nice* woman; she probably belonged to the PTA and the Junior League back home). What had happened was that the husband had convinced the wife they should take off their clothes and then retreat to a shady spot beneath the coconut palms. But when they returned to the beach, they discovered that the tide had washed their clothes away. All I had to offer them to wear were life jackets, but a life jacket wasn't designed to cover what the husband wanted to cover, and as for the wife, by the time I'd helped lift her on board it didn't matter. We both knew each other much better than we'd ever expected—or wanted. During the 45-minute ride back to the marina, conversation was strained. What this story tells us is, don't do dumb things. A boat isn't the only place you can make a fool of yourself, but it is the easiest.

10 Let your listeners do your lying for you: It is generally supposed that all fishermen are liars, which they are, but almost everyone else who works or relaxes around the water is a liar too, so you should be familiar with this method of communicating. Along the waterfront, the most common lies fall into two broad categories: the size of the fish and the severity of the storm. As a Competent Southern Waterperson, it's permissible to lie about both of these things, but it's more in character to intentionally mislead. CSWs prefer to mislead because it requires more skill. Let's use people from Ohio to help illustrate the difference. The walleye is their most commonly lied-about fish, and Lake Erie is their most commonly lied-about body of water. Asked the simple question, "Did you catch anything?" the Ohio waterperson will stretch his hands far apart to describe how big the walleye he didn't catch were. While still holding his hands apart, he will tell you those fish fight like crazy, plus they are the best tasting fish in the world and they normally catch hundreds of them—not that walleye are stupid; oh no, it takes *cunning* to catch them. Then he will tell you about the storm he was in while catching the walleye he didn't really catch: the 10-foot waves and the sleet, which wouldn't have been so bad if the 30-knot winds hadn't brought the fog. Now, let's replace the nonexistent walleye with nonexistent bass, and hear the same question, "Did you catch anything?" posed to a CSW who has just returned from a choppy day on Lake Okeechobee without a single strike. He pauses, sniffs (this is an appropriate time to spit, too, if you're good at it), and says, "Nothing over eight pounds." (Notice—he didn't lie.) Then he adds, "But a person shouldn't keep fish unless he's sure he can eat them, and I had some doubts about whether I'd make it through that storm alive."

Do you see the difference?

Now, if you've read the preceding ten rules, raise your right hand and say, "I have." Good. You are now an official Competent Southern Waterperson. Don't let us down.

The Big Book

My eight-year-old son returned home recently with skinned hands and monofilament fishing line knotted to his back belt loop. I recognized the handiwork of my friend Hoffax.

"He made you do what?"

My son said, "Tied line to me and had me ride off on my bike. About a dozen times. He was checking the drag on his reels."

"Did you get hurt?"

"Naw. It was kind a fun. He only landed me twice."

Hoffax might have been just one more late-1960s drug casualty had an expiration of football eligibility not cut his college career tragically short—an event that snipped all bonds with southpaw politics and dormitory chemistry and cast him into an eerie world that had no halos. He lived in a recreational vacuum for a time before he discovered that a fly rod fit as comfortably into his hand as a Frisbee once had—his brain healing the whole long while. Yet even now, his methods are sometimes unsound.

I made it a point to visit Hoffax that afternoon. He was out the front door before I got up the drive, waving as if to intercept me, grinning as if that might soften my mood. "The boy can flat pedal," he was saying, "I mean, he can *pump* it," which was preface to an explanation of why he had spent the morning reeling in my son. An explanation was unnecessary. I had been through this strange mania with him several years before. We had enlisted motor vehicles to test line strength; used a magnifying glass to check the integrity of knots. We fished 12 hours a day, each and every day, but had never once placed a child in harm's way.

Hoffax said, "One word, just one word," talking like the guy in *The Graduate* who spoke to Dustin Hoffman about plastics. He said, "Tarpon on 4-pound. Can you see it? *Tarpon on 4-pound.*"

This was one word?

"As in *concept*, man."

Like it was something new; as if we hadn't tried it before. I told Hoffax the scars were showing. Chemical mephitism was rearing its ugly head. Therapy, I told him, was indicated here.

"Yanking my son off his bike, for God's sake!"

"He was a willing participant. It was done with a purpose. And it's not like I played him on conventional tackle."

I could guess the purpose. Judging from those eyes, that candent stare, either Nixon was about to resign again or Hoffax was about to make another run at getting his name in The Book.

O O O

First, I should tell you about The Book. Not only will it add ligature to this story, it is a fun thing to know about. The Book is the International Game Fish Association's printing of *World Record Game Fishes*. It is a softback volume, in excess of 300 pages, which lists, species by species, current world-record fish and the names of the people who caught them.

The IGFA is to fishing what the Audubon Society is to birding. It was founded in 1939 by philanthropist Mike Lerner with the help of

Ernest Hemingway and others to establish ethical international fishing regulations and to serve as a processing center for world-record catch data. The organization was privately funded until 1973, when it established various membership categories to help support its own expanded goals: to encourage the study and preservation of fishes around the world. To join as a regular member, you send $20 to: IGFA, 3000 E. Las Olas Blvd., Fort Lauderdale, FL 33316, and in return, you get interesting newsletters, access to the IGFA's excellent research library, and, of course, a copy of The Book.

In The Book are listings of freshwater fish and saltwater fish. There are sharks, splake, bass, barracuda, bullheads, all kinds of trout, all kinds of salmon; hundreds of different species. Many of the fish listed are big, but most of them are not—and that's why, even if you are not an avid angler, you may find The Book of unexpected interest. It is probable that, within a short drive of your home, there is a fish that, if caught within the guidelines of IGFA rules, would enter your name into The Book. Here's why: The IGFA keeps records not only for many species, but for many classes of line strength. An example: The world-record Atlantic salmon taken on 20-pound test line weighed just over 46 pounds. The world record for the same fish, though, in the 50-pound line class is only 13 lbs 8 ounces. So, if you live in Atlantic salmon country and catch a fish that weighs 14 pounds on line that is no stronger than 50-pound test, you've set a world record.

Another example: In the fly rod division, the world record for bluegill in the 8-pound tippet (leader) class is 2 pounds 12 ounces. But the 16-pound record is vacant—no one has ever filed an application. Catch any bluegill on fly rod with a tippet no stronger than 16-pound test, and, if approved, the record is yours.

Simple, huh?

Well, not always. I spoke with Gerry Carr, species research director of the IGFA, about it. "In 1988," he said, "we received 738 applications for world records from around the world, but approved only 437. The applications are put through quite a careful screening process. It's very rare that we find someone is trying to cheat, but we do get the occasional bogus claim. For instance, a man once filed a claim for a largemouth bass, insisting that the fish must have swallowed the diver's weight discovered inside it. More often, though, applications are rejected because IGFA equipment regulations were not followed."

Those regulations are not complicated (they have to do with leader length, length of doubled line, and fishing techniques) and, if you are interested in trying to set a world record, your best bet is to contact the IGFA for a complete listing. All of this adds legitimacy to the record you may someday set and really makes you hone in on knot lore, technique, and the researching of a particular species—a perfect exercise for the beginning angler, and a great study for long winter nights.

And what do you get for your trouble? Well, if your application is accepted you receive a very classy certificate on embossed paper, suitable for framing, and you are qualified to wear a nifty shoulder patch or lapel pin: *IGFA World Record Holder.*

More important, though, you get your name in The Book—until some other fishing hotshot comes along and knocks you and your record out of the saddle.

○ ○ ○

Here is how, several years ago, Hoffax got me involved: I had discovered a shallow water area where, on the strong ebb tide, tarpon stacked near an oyster bar to feed. I had jumped several large fish (all over 100 pounds) on fly rod when Hoffax turned suddenly to me and said, "Do you realize that if we landed any one of those fish on 4-pound test, our names would probably be in the record book forever? Not just a couple of years, man; I mean *forever.*"

"Yeah, but we couldn't."

"Why not?"

"Four-pound is too light. We could never set the hook."

"Do you know that? Have you ever tried?"

"Well, no . . . "

"It would be something your great-grandkids could read about. We're talking immortality here. Maybe even a spot on Letterman. And you'd get your name in The Book."

Well, immortality is a heady lure, and the next day we returned to the spot with 4-pound test spooled on small spinning reels. To my surprise, Hoffax hooked a fish and then fought it for more than an hour before losing it.

"That guy musta gone 140 pounds!"

Then I hooked a fish and fought it for nearly three hours before it finally jumped and spit the lure. My shoulders ached; my jaw creaked from its attention to the long drama, but I felt good.

"You know, Hoffax, we really could do this."

"For sure, man!"

That day fired a dull interest that, over the next few weeks, blazed into a world-record mania to which, later, I vowed never to fall victim again. We were up each morning in darkness, on the water before sunrise, fishing and fighting big fish all day without ever landing a thing. I became fanatical about tying perfect knots. Badly tied knots weaken line and, with line so light, we could entertain no flaws. Hoffax said we should use a microscope; instead, I bought a good magnifying glass and, at night, when I should have been sleeping, I stayed up late, hunched over spools of line, peering through the glass like some pathetic Swiss watchmaker.

After about five days of this, I said, "The problem is, we need to hook a fish that weighs under 100 pounds. These fish are just too big. They head for deep water and we can't lift them."

Hoffax said, "You know what the real problem is? We let them *get* to deep water. We need to find a way to gauge optimum drag for all situations: the strike, the first few really fast runs; find the point of maximum drag and maybe we can slow those big boys down."

Instead of taking us onto the water, that project took us into the street. Astonished passersby would slow to watch as I stood in the middle of the road, rod bowed, line tied to the bumper of my old Toyota, while Hoffax banged through the gears and raced away. I made notes. We tested various knots. We burned a lot of fuel. We looked like idiots. And Hoffax would say things like, "Do those people have their names in The Book? Hell no. Those folks don't have a *clue.*"

The closest we came to setting the world record was on a tarpon that had to weigh in excess of 120 pounds. Hoffax fought it for 4 hours, 27 minutes, the two of us following that wide-bodied creature through the tendrils of a twilight lightning storm and then into darkness. Twice he had the fish close enough for me to actually touch the long leader . . . but then the traumatized line parted.

I could have cried.

We didn't fish the next two days because of a storm front, and when we finally did get out, the tarpon had moved from that spot. We motored around looking for other fish, and happened onto a school of big jack crevalles feeding. We had plenty of ultralight line ready, so we practiced on those fish—and each set world records later approved by the IGFA: Hoffax on 2-pound, me on 4-pound tippet fly rod.

We each got our names in The Book—though both records were to be broken again within three years.

Which is why, I guessed now, looking at Hoffax, he wanted to try it again.

"Hoffax, I'm not going through another two weeks like the last time. Working with that light line is like trying to tie knots with spider web. My eyes can't take it."

"Have you seen the new Book, man? Have you seen it? Every fish we had on was bigger than the current record, and I've got all the little details soaped. See, your boy on his bike can do what no car can do. He can shift and weave, man; he can juke-step through the grass, just like a fish. *That's* the way to set drag. We're talking window of opportunity here."

The Big Book

For the first time in a long time, I looked at the listings ... all of those names from all over the world ... all of those exotic species of fish dutifully recorded ... holding the weight of The Book in my hands, the lone permanent artifact of a sport that lacks only permanency.

My son was amenable. He didn't mind. In fact, he said it was kind of fun.

Coming to America

ey West, midnight, and the island dead-enders and drug freaks roam the docks with blazing eyes. They have come to see the Cuban-Americans readying their small boats for the 110-mile Gulf Stream journey to Mariel Harbor, Cuba, where people of their blood await rescue.

And, like some indefinable affront, the face of bravery creates an odd uneasiness among those of us who watch.

Goin' for their relatives, but they'll come back with crooks. . . . Cubanos are crazy—them boats are too small.

Even the fishing guides guarding their gear on charter-boat row react to it, laughing nervously like outlanders come to town. The novelty of these heroics in an America subjugated by rat-tat news reports and film at 11 of screw-ups, goon-ups, blazing helicopters, mealy-mouthed presidents, and blindfolded hostages seems to make strangers of us all. And the grim bond of ethnic jokes is permeated by a vague bitterness akin to envy.

The next afternoon, April 27, a freak squall hit the Straits of Florida:

hurricane-force winds, gusts to 80 knots, thunderheads trailing from the west-northwest. The Key West Coast Guard received more than 100 distress calls and spent the next days searching for skiffs and bodies awash. One of the calls came from two Cuban-American friends of mine, their sailboat smashed on a reef. Later they would provide me with cause for going. Could I get a boat? Could I get them to Mariel? We departed on Monday, May 5, three days after the news of the failure of the Iranian hostage rescue left a nation muttering between headlines and a few hundred of us sailing in the Freedom Flotilla with the dazed uncertainty of stray dogs.

○   ○   ○

FIRST DAY, GULF STREAM   The first thing you see approaching Cuba from open sea is a low bank of cumulus clouds appearing, on the curve of horizon, like a sudden Dakota windscape. The sea is a mile deep, purple-black in shafts of clear light, and flying fish lift in coveys before you, skimming cresting waves and luminous sargassum weed like locusts. We arrived at dawn. Clouds were fire-laced to the southeast and, later, the bleak facades of factories and pre-Castro high-rise hotels below Havana caught the light in a blaze of geometrics. Mariel Harbor, debarkation point for Cuban refugees, was 23 miles to the west, a surge of dark cliffs.

We left Key West yesterday. Cuban-Americans who couldn't afford the $10,000 to $50,000 to charter a commercial vessel continued to unload and provision their frail skiffs at the docks at Garrison Bight, and newspapers continued to report their sinkings. All night long I tracked them on our passage across the Straits of Florida: a long night of rolling sea, small-boat distress calls, assurances from the Coast Guard cutter *Dallas,* and the glimmer of running lights in the ocean darkness. But we had an easy time of it—15 hours, and the Cuban gunboats at the mouth of Mariel Harbor have just now come into sight.

Our own boat is a 50-foot grouper fisherman, white fiberglass over wood with a single screw GMC diesel, called *Misfit II,* with a Tampa registry. It came outfitted with Loran C, twin white-line recorders, VHF radio, and a 22-year-old drug-seared half-wit pilot none of us wanted—but had to accept. The vessel is owned by the friend of a friend who insisted on having a hand in matters. There are six of us aboard, the most important of whom are my Cuban-American friends Ernesto and Jeffrey. The two of them have had a tough time of it, the wear evident when we picked them up yesterday at Truman Annex docks in Key West. They have lost a boat, almost lost their lives, and have spent the past week living hand to mouth in a frantic last-ditch effort to secure enough cash to get them to Mariel. Both are close to the edge.

Jeffrey is 24, earnest, so sensitive as to seem frail; a fine photographer-writer who looks like a cross between Redford and the angular collegians who pose for those Arrow shirt ads. And because he is blond, he has been privy to all the ethnic slurs in earlier negotiations with the shrimp-boat mercenaries. No veteran of bar-fight lingo, Jeff later expressed his rage rather awkwardly. "I just wanted to grab them by the cheeks and shake them. I wanted to scream, '*I'm* a Cuban!'" He has certainly proved his devotion to heritage in the past weeks. In his quest he has abandoned his job and his fiancée and lost the boat he had sailed twice across the Atlantic and loved well. And he has never even met the paternal relatives—a man, a wife, and two young daughters—he seeks to bring from Cuba. "We have the same blood," he explained. "They'd do the same for me."

At 39, Ernesto is equally dedicated. He grew up in upper-middle-class Havana and, at age 19, fled Cuba when his father, who was a sports columnist for the newspaper *El Mundo,* was labeled a traitor by the Castro regime for a story criticizing its handling of a car race.

"That was in 1960," Ernesto said. "A few months after we left, the Communist party took over the newspaper. My father and I went to work on *El Mundo in Exile* in Miami. My mother and sister were supposed to follow us to America. We waited and waited but they never arrived. Castro had refused them visas to punish my father. I cannot describe the horror we felt when we finally knew."

When Castro removed his guards from the gates of the Peruvian embassy outside Havana and announced that "anyone unhappy with the struggle for socialism" was welcome to leave Cuba, Ernesto got a five-word telegram from his mother: PLEASE COME AND GET US.

O O O

SECOND DAY, MARIEL HARBOR   This is a huge inland lake of a harbor umbilicaled to the sea by a natural deep-water channel. The east side of the port is cliffed, industrialized—cement factory, power plant, tapered verticals of smokestacks throwing an acid smog across us and the 1,500 other shrimp boats, sloops, skiffs, and cruisers anchored alone or rafted in makeshift communities, all waiting. The factories give way to higher cliffs and growths of bamboo, yellow against the deeper green of royal palm and ficus, and on the highest ridge is the Cuban Naval Academy, like a stone castle. We are anchored on the west side of the harbor a few hundred yards from a peninsula on which is a military outpost. From my seat atop the wheelhouse, I watch guards in baggy khaki patrol the beach with German shepherds; another patrols on horseback, barefoot. Beyond the barracks is a small aircraft control tower with an amphibious landing strip and a steel wharf for gunboats. Best of all there's a baseball diamond, backstopped with chicken wire, and we watch the soldiers play.

This morning we were boarded by an officious Cuban officer with the unlikely name of Captain Lobo. He made a token inspection of our boat, took the lists of relatives (with addresses, in triplicate) whom Ernesto and Jeffrey are requesting, then left with the promise that we would be leaving with all relatives—and 100 other refugees—within three or four days. So we have spent the afternoon nursing a guarded optimism: Ernesto paces the deck, watching through binoculars the slow refugee-loading process across the harbor at Pier Three. Billy, the pilot, victim of mid-1970s bad chemistry, sits in the wheelhouse chain-smoking and reading his *Hustler*. Hervey-John and Westy, two of my best friends, juggle tennis balls on the aft deck, teaching Jeffrey. All of us have heard the rumors that in Mariel soldiers find lying easier than telling the truth.

○　○　○

MIDNIGHT　Tonight on VHF channel 16 we listened to the captain of the vessel *Patty Paige* call his home in the United States via Key West marine operator. You could hear the captain's wife plainly, but every time he tried to talk, the frequency was overpowered by a shrill electronic buzz like that of a dentist's drill. The Cubans were jamming him.

"Honey, is that you? I can't hear you."

"Yeah, I'm in Mariel . . ." *buzz-z-z-z-z-z.*

"What was that, darling?"

"I said . . ." *buzz-z-z-z-z-z.*

The captain of the *Patty Paige* tried two more calls home, and by the time he gave up, his wife was in tears. When it was over, we all moved separately from the wheelhouse, filled with silent outrage.

"Welcome to Castro's Cuba," Ernesto said.

○　○　○

THIRD DAY　Early this morning Jeffrey and Ernesto took a government taxi boat ($10 one way) to Pier Two, where, they have been told, it is possible to catch a special bus to the Triton Hotel in Havana and call the relatives we have come to pick up. Hot morning, no wind. Smog hangs over the harbor like a cloud. This boat smells of fish and rancid squid baits; flies have found us—quick little devils, too. Anchored nearby is an old converted Russian whaling ship with a hand-painted sign: *Venta de Agua*. Boats line up behind it to pay $1 a gallon for fresh water. The harbor is full of American boats cruising aimlessly, anchoring and reanchoring. Waiting. Waiting. Westy and Hervey-John are polishing a juggling act that could take them far if Ed Sullivan were still alive. Westy is muscled, red-haired, Viking-like.

Hervey-John is part bear, part savant, with quick hands and a master's degree. Our friendships are linked by mutual Southern origins, but also by interests that go beyond beer and Copenhagen snuff. I find their presence comforting.

From across the water and the maze of boats comes the smell of meat frying and the sound of thin laughter edged with hysteria. A patrol boat with armed guards approaches and, silly with boredom, Westy juggles for them while Hervey-John bellows like a ringmaster: "Now ladies and gentlemen, all the way from Fort Myers, Florida, just for your juggling pleasure . . ."

One of the soldiers lifts his scythe-clipped Russian AK-47 assault rifle and takes aim at Westy. The weapon kicks four times with mock fire, and the other guards burst into laughter as the tennis balls bounce to the deck in disarray.

Flushed, now ignoring the guards, Westy retrieves the balls stoically and begins to juggle again. Cuban-Americans on boats anchored near ours applaud him politely.

○ ○ ○

FOURTH DAY, 2 A.M. Days are strange here. Nights are stranger. Searchlights sweep the harbor and boats in the distance stand out in blue silhouette through factory smog and vacillating darkness. Last night there was a sudden siren and muted gunfire from the military outpost. Who could they have been shooting at? A Cuban citizen trying to swim to a Freedom Flotilla boat? At least one Cuban soldier has already been killed in such an attempt. No way for us to know.

Jeffrey and Ernesto returned from Havana with rum and the official newspaper, *Granma*. Ernesto's telephone conversation with his mother had put him on the verge of tears. Cubans claimed by Freedom Flotilla people are being abused by Castro's neighborhood spy groups—beatings, arson. A few days ago a busload of Castro thugs attacked a line of refugees outside the U.S. Interests Section with baseball bats and tire irons. Many were seriously injured. Ernesto's mother and sister still want to leave. But none of the relatives has yet been contacted by Cuban authorities, so we will be here at least three more days. Captain Lobo, the lying dog, was wrong. Ernesto is a nervous, pacing wreck. His intensity is anything but irritating—it helps combat the boredom we all feel with a reminder of purpose.

Granma, printed in English, described how the refugee "parasites" were being mistreated after reaching America. According to *Granma,* 200 refugee children were intentionally burned to death, and U.S. Marines are greeting new arrivals in Key West with rocks. One editorial ended: ". . . and we the Fighting People of the Great Revolution cannot rest until we break the backs of the American Imperialists, ever, ever." As a well-meaning product of late-1960s political southpawism, I find myself sliding inexorably, if not lickety-split, toward the military right. The nerve of those Commies.

Tonight Westy, Jeffrey, Hervey-John, and I took a taxi boat to Pier Two with its dirt row of plywood booths where, at great expense, you can buy Hatuey beer, rum, green cigars, food, or even fighting cocks. We were the only Anglos there and the Cuban-Americans gave us wide berth until—we learned later—they realized we weren't Russians. After that there were no strangers, only kindred spirits: Americans trapped in Mariel. Blatant patriotism hardly appeals to me, but tonight it was welcomed. The four of us found ourselves the focal point of conversation and free beer: the symbols of something that went out of vogue with *Sands of Iwo Jima,* or was bled to death by Vietnam, Nixon, and the Iranians. A regal Cuban-American named Jorge, who wore a braided captain's cap and a handlebar mustache, took me aside after many beers to denounce Barbara Walters for the cozy interview she did with Castro, and to tell me why he came to Mariel.

"I did not come to Mariel to pick up criminals and fiends," he said. "I came to get my daughter—but if I must take back criminals to get her, then I will."

He pointed to the high cliff above us and the harbor. "I was a student at the Naval Academy before I escaped Cuba. And I saw Castro line up his 'enemies of the revolution' on that cliff and shoot them off." His voice choked momentarily. "My own father was executed on that cliff—and that is why I will do anything to get my daughter out of Cuba, amigo. I will die before I leave without her."

○ ○ ○

SIXTH DAY, HAVANA   The 22-story Triton Hotel—only a dozen blocks from the Peruvian embassy—has become a hotbed of rumor, a bleak depot for the weary and the desperate. The lobby is thick with cigarette smoke and human motion. Cuban-Americans stand in line outside the narrow *comunicación* room to phone their relatives or wire the States for more money. Money is what Mariel Harbor is all about: After a disastrous year for sugarcane and tobacco crops, the Castro regime is supposedly making a half million American dollars a day on the Freedom Flotilla.

Westy and I took a bus to the Triton this afternoon and were immediately in trouble. Stupidly, we had forgotten to unbelt our fishing knives before leaving the boat. As we entered the lobby, an armed guard shoved us roughly aside, and all I could think was: *They've spotted my tape recorder and they're going to hear what Jorge said about Barbara Walters and Castro, and I'm going to spend the next 50 years playing one-on-one with rats in some Cuban prison.* But it was our knives they took—two fine Gerbers. In my imagination, at least, the potential for violence here is like some cold malevolence, fed by constant rumors. Already new acquaintances have told us of Americans being hauled off secretly to Cuban jails, of suicides, of outlandish fines. The most frightening rumor is that Castro might seal off the harbor and hold us all hostage unless Carter agrees to shut down our Guantánamo military base. I know some of the rumors to be true; others I suspect of being complete lies. Yet, here at the Triton Hotel, where we are caged in by soldiers and barbed wire, all rumors hit you with equal impact.

Luckily, we have been adopted by Miguel Herrera, a reassuring young man from Miami. Miguel has invited us to shower and stay in his hotel room, where I now record this. Hervey-John and Westy watch a Russian soap opera with Spanish subtitles on a Russian-built television set. Miguel is 21 stories below, trying to call the brother he hopes to take to America. I stand here drip-drying on the bare tile floor trying to sort out characters and impressions. Friendships in this hotel are made summarily—with no better criterion than a lost look or the color of your hair. In a crowded hallway, for instance, I collided with a stocky black guy wearing a San Antonio Spurs T-shirt. He backed away, eyes wide, then grinned at me like a long-lost teammate. "Never thought I'd be saying this, but it sure is good to see a dude with blond hair!" His name was Barry and he had gone shrimping to make money for college, and the next thing he knew, his boat was headed for Mariel. "What the hell us Americans doin' in Cuba?" he kept asking.

On the way to the outdoor bar, Barry and I acquired another of the lost and lonely—a tall beachboy from Cedar Rapids named Derk. Derk was a precipitate of Mariel Harbor paranoia ("Been here 22 days, man, and I don't mind sayin' that morale on my boat is at an all-time low"). He was filled with rumors and grisly parallels. The outdoor bar is separated from the beach by a chain-link fence; soldiers loitered outside the fence, watching several hundred Cuban-Americans milling around inside. "Read the papers," Derk said. "They're taking American hostages in Iran, South America—you name it. The world used to respect America; Americans used to respect their government. But no more, not since Carter. Those Cubans said you'd be leaving in three days? Baloney. You'll be here till all your food and money are gone, then they'll load your boat with all the human dregs Castro doesn't want and tell you to come back a *second* time if you want relatives. They're not afraid of America anymore; they've got us right where they want us. Look at those one-man gun towers outside the fence. Recognize them? Just like a Nazi concentration camp. And they're all built to shoot right down into this enclosure. We're sitting ducks, man. Don't forget it."

Batfishing in the Rainforest

O   O   O

CONVERSATION WITH MIGUEL   "I went to an elementary school of the Revolution before I was taken to America. When I was in the fourth grade, our teacher came into the classroom one day and told us to close our eyes and, if we wanted ice cream, to pray to God and ask him for it. I liked ice cream, so I did as she said. But when we opened our eyes, there was no ice cream. 'Remember this,' our teacher told us. And then she said we should close our eyes and pray to Fidel for ice cream. When we opened our eyes this time, there was a large tray of ice cream before us. And our teacher told us, 'Remember this most of all.' And I remembered, amigo. I will always remember the fear I felt then."

O   O   O

SEVENTH DAY, PIER THREE   This is the heart of the goings and comings of Mariel Harbor: an expanse of cement wharf heavily armed and guarded by soldiers where the refugees and the American boats are finally joined. Above me, from the third floor of a concrete building, a soldier scans the harbor with powerful binoculars, a heavy machine gun at his elbow. The refugees wait in a long single-file line in the heat, expressionless. One by one, the guards search them, taking all jewelry and baggage. Like us, the refugees seem to be in slight shock from an incident that has just occurred. As Westy, Hervey-John, and I watched, a slightly built man raised mild protestations as a guard tried to take the wedding band from his left hand. Another guard rushed forward and hit him in the teeth with the butt of his assault rifle so quickly that it seemed, for a moment, I might be imagining it. The refugees in line near him moved only enough to get the man back to his feet and wipe the chips of teeth and blood from his ruined mouth—the implications obvious: If he did not stand, he would not be loaded.

Long moments later, still mesmerized, the three of us realized that someone was yelling at us over a loudspeaker. It was a Cuban soldier:

What were we doing on Pier Three? Were we loading? If not, we must leave immediately. Suddenly, through the chaos came the imposing figure of Jorge, my friend from Pier Two—handlebar mustache, captain's cap, and all. He was smiling, eating a sandwich. "Do you know what that soldier just told me? He told me to 'get those gringos out of here.' " He chuckled, amused but bitter. "They don't mind if we Cuban-Americans see it, but they don't want you to."

Jorge found a friend with a skiff who said he would take us back to our boat. When I tried to thank him, Jorge stopped me short. "You are the first Anglos I have met who did not come to Mariel to get rich," he said. "I would carry you to your boat on my back if I had to." Strangely, Jorge's kindness, the kindness of Miguel, and the appreciation of Jeffrey and Ernesto, too, have only served to make me feel a fraud. In slow-motion replay, I see the rifle butt colliding again and again with the mouth of the poor man who stands a hundred feet from me; and I sense, in the moment, a grim fusion of truth: Of the thousands in Mariel Harbor, I am neither honest liberator nor honest mercenary. One in a nation shamed by its own headlines, I have come, it seems, to freeload on the grand gesture of others—fascinated by their bravery and envious of their union. I feel as if I have come just to watch that man fall bleeding, only to rise again.

○ ○ ○

EVENING, *MISFIT II* After the paranoia of Havana and Pier Three, this 50-foot boat is almost like home. Everybody seems charged by a sense of reunion. Jeffrey slapped my shoulder and said, "When you guys didn't come back last night, I thought the Gestapo had you for sure." Jeff seems to be holding up pretty well—he joins in our juggling and practical jokes, and he even tries a dip of our Copenhagen snuff, thereby sacrificing his supper. But Ernesto becomes increasingly worn. He listens to VHF 16 day and night, hoping the authorities will call our boat, and his pure Basque face is lined, worried. When he discovered that we had been to Pier Three, he immediately wanted to know everything about the place. His first questions were general, tentative, but then he finally asked what he really wanted to know.

"Back in Key West, I heard so much about the brutality at the loading dock—Pier Three. But there are so many rumors."

"From what we saw, the guards were pretty polite and businesslike."

He sighed, relieved. He said he was glad because his mother was a very delicate woman and could not tolerate violence.

O O O

EIGHTH DAY   Typical morning in Mariel Harbor. Bored. Waiting. We juggle, then compose a song on steel pots, add lyrics, and call it *Mariel Harbor Blues*. Billy, the drug zombie, chain-smokes and reads his *Hustler* for the hundredth time. Ernesto paces. Earlier a man came by in a small boat and offered his wife and his daughter as prostitutes. He said he was desperate for money; the soldiers had told him that if he could hold out in the harbor for only a few more days, he would get his relatives.

O O O

NINTH DAY, 2 A.M.   In Mariel you learn pacing. You start drinking seriously at dusk so the searchlights and sirens will not keep you awake at bedtime. Tonight, as in Havana, I felt the Mariel paranoia move through me like a fever: What if they did seal off the harbor? What if they did try to hold us hostage? Hervey-John, Westy, and I sat up discussing it. By the time we had finished, we all knew which boat at the military outpost we would steal, and which guards we would have to kill.

O O O

MAY 15, THURSDAY   Suddenly, it's over. Word came by radio this morning: Carter has ordered all American vessels to leave Mariel Harbor *without* refugees. For Ernesto and Jeffrey, it couldn't have come at a worse time—they had just learned that their relatives would be ready to load within four days. They are in shock, too stunned to cry. Ernesto moves about the boat in a daze, catatonic. What Jimmy Carter and his cohorts don't understand is that you just can't pull anchor and wave good-bye to the guards. You leave with refugees or the gunboats intercept you.

So again we wait at Pier Three. From my seat atop the wheelhouse, I watch the chaotic activity and the people who seek freedom: hundreds upon hundreds of them, three lines curving along the cement wharf, stoic in the dismal heat and factory haze. Old men, women, and children; convicts and, no doubt, Castro agents, standing anonymously and shoulder to shoulder with the myriad others who seek America like a dream. And if it was bad for those of us who waited, what they have gone through is unimaginable. A little girl, age nine perhaps, holds the hand of her father as they stand in line. She has long brown hair and fawn eyes. I wave—she smiles. I wink, she winks back, then covers her eyes, shy. I worry for her, for all of them. What are those without American relatives going to do, where will they go? And what is America, already stumbling with heavy welfare rolls and unemployment, going to do with more than 125,000 non-English-speaking refugees? I take three tennis balls and juggle for her. She claps her hands, eyes wide, grinning.

○ ○ ○

MIDNIGHT, GULF STREAM, HOMEWARD BOUND Wind. Rolling black sea. A flying fish breaks water, dripping green phosphorescence. It crashes back into the darkness like a falling star. One hundred and sixty-five refugees roll and struggle with the boat—they reek of vomit, steam of body heat. A low groan. Ernesto and Jeffrey try to help the sick. They carry kitchen pots from person to person, dumping the upchuck overboard. Westy lies huddled beneath a tarp with a man who bears the tattooed numerals of a Cuban convict upon his chest. Hervey-John cradles the little boy who wears his gift: a Kansas City Royals cap. The girl with the fawn eyes, Aurora, sleeps in my arms. She moans, flinches—dreaming. Before leaving Pier Three, a Cuban officer confirmed what Ernesto feared most: If we didn't ignore Carter's orders, his mother and sister and the rest would never be sent to America. With their homes already confiscated, they would go to a labor camp. Or prison.

○ ○ ○

MORNING, AMERICAN WATERS We pass the huge Coast Guard cutter *Dallas* off to port, and a young Cuban, still pale with seasickness, eyes it suspiciously.

"Russian?" he asks me.

I feel a surge of emotion, ridiculously close to tears. "American," I tell him.

He grins and raises an ecstatic clenched fist. "*Estados Unidos!*" He breathes deeply, watching the lordly *Dallas* disappear. And then he begins the chant, water rolling down his cheeks. And one by one the other refugees join in: "*Libertad . . . Libertad . . . LIBERTAD!*"

With Key West a thin smudge, cloudlike on the horizon, we are home.

○ ○ ○

POSTSCRIPT The Castro government proved itself to be at least an occasional victim of its own bureaucratic discord and the general confusion in Mariel. A week after our return, the mother of Ernesto and the paternal relatives of Jeffrey arrived unexpectedly in Key West. Someone at Pier Three had failed to notice their forgotten names on some forgotten list.

Lessons in
White-Water Style

et's say you are articulate, intelligent, rational—yet persist in paddling white water anyway. Let's say you've abandoned the headline rivers of the West for the folklore rivers of the South; places of shadow and mist such as the Chattooga of Georgia, the Ocoee of Tennessee, the Buffalo River of Arkansas. Let's say you've made your way through the great Smoky Mountains to the western ledge of North Carolina for a shot at the Nantahala River, a day-long dam surge of big water that blows noise and cold wind through the forest canopy and high up onto the far dark ridges. Maybe you're an expert; maybe you're an advanced paddler—either way, you've acquired all the accepted artifacts of expertise: high-tech Kevlar or Royalex canoe, multicolored Extrasport PFD, thick plastic flotation bags, high-impact plastic helmet, and maybe a hand-made wooden Silver Creek paddle thrown in for style. In other words, you know your sport, paid your dues, know the ropes—all that sort of stuff.

Batfishing in the Rainforest

Now, you're at the Nantahala, at Ferebee Park, waiting to put in, waiting to put all this nice gear and expertise to work, when up pulls a pickup truck and two guys get out who, judging from that tinny clatter coming from the back seat, enjoy canned beverages. One of the guys has muscles and a shaved head; the other guy has a head that would look better shaved, and lashed to the top of their pickup is a square-sterned aluminum canoe and a cheap fiberglass canoe (decorated with a quaint birchbark pattern) of a sort sometimes donated to summer camps for inner-city youths.

This is unusual and interesting, so you watch as these guys consider the river for a moment, then—impressed, perhaps, by the distant roar—select the aluminum canoe. From the bed of the truck, they take two wooden paddles and then two orange things, which, after a moment, you recognize as a kind of inflatable flotation vest occasionally pilfered from shabby Central American airlines. They have no helmets, but they do pull on hats—one reads *Omaha Vaccine Company Field Tester.*

Are they actually going to run the Nantahala with this junk?

By now, other paddlers are watching as the two guys wrestle their canoe to the bank, and one of them dips his toe in as if testing bathwater and says, "Man, this river is *cold.*" To which the other replies automatically, "Yeah, and it's deep, too," which illustrates how much attention one pays to the other.

Yep, they're going to try and run it.

Now, the questions posed to you, the experienced white-water paddler, are:

(A) Judging from their abysmal lack of proper equipage, do you assume these two are imbeciles and warn them of the danger they will soon face?

(B) Do you assume they are experienced eccentrics on the cutting edge of their craft and bid them Godspeed?

(C) Do you break into their truck and enjoy some of those tasty canned beverages, since the ambulance drivers aren't going to waste time stopping for personal effects anyway.

Well, the answer is A. But everyone at Ferebee Park failed that day. When my friend with the shaved head and I got into the aluminum canoe, no one so much as even waved good-bye.

○ ○ ○

If there is a lesson here, it has to do with equipage vs. "styleage," and what these two confusing things imply.

For our purposes, let us say equipage is that which is essential to pursuing a sport in a safe and effective manner. Let us also say that styleage (a word that should be included in dictionaries) is that which, in the highest echelons of certain sports, may complement expertise but, in most cases, better indicates one's passion for a sport and, sometimes, the depth of one's pocketbook. Equipage is a staff. Styleage is a flag.

For instance: For weekend joggers, well-designed running shoes are equipage; racing flats and noisy public displays of carbo loading are styleage. For amateur skiers, warm clothing and safe bindings are equipage; cowboy hats designed in wind tunnels are styleage. For travelers, Lomotil tablets and clean socks are equipage; safari jackets and shirts with epaulets are pure styleage.

You get the idea. Now, if you also get the impression styleage is a better indicator of snob quotient than expertise, you are no doubt right—but only sometimes. Not long ago, while visiting Philadelphia, I was invited by some people to watch a bicycle race. We would pedal to the course, they said. I arrived at the rendezvous to find the entire group clothed in bright spandex riding shorts, Campagnolo hats, tinted goggles, and Coolmax jerseys emblazoned with foreign phrases— French, perhaps, or maybe Italian. Had I known *we* were going to race, I said, I wouldn't have worn jeans and combat boots. Oh, but we weren't racing, I was told—we would just be watching. I almost asked why, then, were they attired as if to participate in the *Tour de South Street*, but a rare chivalric lapse stopped me. I'm glad. These people weren't snobs, and I noticed no hint of pretension in their approach to their sport. They didn't mind going slow so I could keep up, and I received no evil snickers when my boot lodged in the stirrup of my borrowed bike and I tipped over at a stoplight. Yet, while their clothing was functional, it was clearly not worn for function—it was worn as a declaration of style. We, they were telling other spectators at the race, are cyclists too. They were waving a banner, declaring their fidelity.

Now, there's nothing malicious in this. In an amorphous world, uniforms (and that is what styleage is) add a splash of color; assert one's identity and standing. Styleage provides ego satisfaction, especially in those sports that are essentially private; sports in which one's expertise cannot be publicly assessed. But problems can arise out of a form of dual snobbery. Someone not stylishly outfitted might be incorrectly judged to be a boob, a jerk, a neophyte grit-slinger. Seen from the other side, someone nattily outfitted might be unfairly pronounced a snob, a rich snot, a motherless pork-barrel-sucking hound. It can get ugly.

But the real dangers become manifest when the neophyte confuses equipage with styleage—and the borders *are* sometimes murky. Maybe you don't need Poly-Pag mesh cycling shoes to enjoy biking, but maybe you do need a neoprene Farmer John to surf effectively. Maybe you don't need anodized rails and Lexan seats on a cruising canoe, or maybe it's all just a marketing ruse designed for snob appeal and you don't need any of it. When confusion begins to cloak judgment, two things can happen, both bad: The neophyte can decide (1) there's no sense trying to play without a uniform, or (2) to hell with all uniforms.

That day on the Nantahala, my friend and I said to hell with the uniform—not through reverse snobbery, but through naïveté, lack of experience, and general dumbness.

Lessons in White-Water Style

My friend, who is a former Marine combat surgeon and should know better, refuses to shoulder all the blame.

"Why are all those people wearing helmets?" he asked as we made our first tentative strokes into the current.

"Because they don't own ball caps?" I offered.

This, he still insists, was an intentionally obscure answer.

○   ○   ○

A hundred yards or so below Ferebee Park, the Nantahala River makes an abrupt right turn, the current caroming off a wooded embankment, bringing the paddler, if he is still in his boat, face to face with Delebar's Rock, the first of several big rapids on the three-mile run to Nantahala Falls and the Nantahala Outdoor Center below.

It is an exciting thing to see one's first rapid from the thin husk of a canoe, but it is even more exciting when that canoe has already flooded and flipped, and one is dog-paddling along beside it—which I was. I don't know what happened. One moment we were pounding along, the next moment we were in the water. This was a disappointment. At the canoe ramp, I had been frightened at the prospect of seeing Delebar's Rock. Now I was frightened because I couldn't see it, the vantage point of bobbing up and down, up and down, being visually unsatisfactory. But it didn't impair my hearing. I could hear that damned rapid getting louder and louder, and it was like being sucked into an all-day train wreck.

As a professional outdoorsman, I did have the presence of mind to try and take the rapids feetfirst. That lasted until I hit the first rock, and then I was tumbling, tumbling, until I finally lodged up against something and forced my head to the surface to take stock: I was in the middle of the river, in only about three feet of water, and I still had my paddle. So far, so good. Where my friend was was his business. Survival is the ultimate definition of democracy, and I wasn't about to abandon the ideal for which so many of his patients had valiantly fought. The river was blowing past me like a bad wind, but, using the paddle as a brace, I battled my way to my feet. This seemed like a victory until I realized that, if I took a step, the current would sweep me into the next rapid below. That's when I remembered the inflatable vest. I reached for the cord that would activate the CO_2 cartridge—but then had a horrible thought: What if it didn't inflate? Wearing a vest that might work was a comfort; wearing a vest that didn't work would be almost too much to bear, and no one knew its shabby antecedents better than I who had stolen it. A PFD from a Belizean Tri-Star could not be trusted. Yet it was absurd not to *try* . . . but then my foot slipped, and I didn't have to think about it anymore, because I was tumbling again.

Somehow I reached the bank. I lay there like a beached whale, looking up into faces I didn't recognize, blinking dully at their questions. "Hey, man, you okay? You need a doctor or something?"

I got shakily to my feet and peered down river. "I had one around here someplace. A guy with a shaved head." Then I saw the glint of the aluminum canoe, gray in the mountain light, pitching through the current while my friend clung to it. I watched until he made it safely to shore.

"Now I know why you wanted to use my canoe," he said when I arrived with the pickup to get him. His boat looked as if it had spent a year in a K mart parking lot. "It's got *holes* in it. We're talking scrap metal."

Later, I spoke with Marc Hunt of the Nantahala Outdoor Center, a place that serves great food and is staffed by people who give good advice. I told Hunt, who is treasurer of the co-op that owns and operates the center, what had happened, and he immediately made me feel better about my bad judgment.

"My first white-water experience was almost exactly like that," he told me. "Back in the early '70s, a friend and I decided we could learn the strokes on our own, and we didn't give much thought to equipment. We used what we could afford. We put his aluminum canoe in on the Conasauga River in southeastern Tennessee, and I mean we *to-taled* it on a rock. I got trapped underwater for what seemed a long time, but I got out. I came fairly close to dying that day. I was a little gun-shy after that, but we still had this burning desire to paddle white water, so we began to talk to people who really knew what they were doing. They told us what we did need and what we didn't need, and that's how we learned. I've been paddling ever since. But I'll tell you what, no experience in my career was as thrilling as that first time on the Conasauga in that aluminum canoe. But I don't recommend that approach to anyone because paddling white water is inherently risky."

I told Marc about my equipage versus styleage theory, and he agreed that distinguishing between the two can be difficult. "In sports like white water and mountain climbing, though," he said, "most of the equipment is not only functional, it's a necessity. It's not a matter of looking good. It's a matter of staying alive."

Navy SEALs

*The cowards never started, and the weak
died along the way.*

—Engraving outside
NAVY SEAL training center

f one really wanted to get in shape, I reasoned, one should eschew those Yuppie workout programs designed by and for a vagarious cast of bad actors, dilettante athletes, and other trendy glitzoids. It was my belief that chain-smoker Jane Fonda is to health what Jim Bakker is to religion; that Sylvester Stallone is to fitness what Buck Rogers is to space travel. To discover how to get in shape, I decided, one should avoid those who sell exercise for profit and seek the advice of those for whom conditioning is a necessity of life. Which is how I ended up at the Naval Special Warfare Center at Coronado, California, on the beach at 5 a.m., with trainees for the Navy's elite SEAL (Sea, Air, Land) commando team.

The morning's evolution (a Navy word for exercise), trainees were told, was a two-mile boat ride into the Pacific, then a predawn swim back. Oh yeah, then a nice three-mile beach jog; not too fast because tomorrow they'd be doing a four-mile run in jungle boots, in sand, for time—everyone under 30 minutes. Then, after classes, they'd get down to some serious physical training (PT). Serious PT for the SEALs normally includes running up and down the beach carrying telephone poles, then an obstacle course—a 21-station emetic that looks as if it had been designed by devil dogs from hell. Just another day in the eight-month training routine.

The instructor was saying, "Ready gentlemen? Good tight swim line, and push it. It's only two miles, so we want everyone in by sunrise."

From the darkness, trainees replied, "Hoo-YAH!"—an answer that lacks definition or reason, so was the perfect response, considering the circumstances.

I found all of this impressive, but troubling too, because in a moment of pure lunacy, some irrational goof had insisted that I be allowed to work out with the trainees. A liability waiver had even been signed—by me, the irrational goof. Have you ever been on Coronado Beach at 5 a.m.? It's dark, it's cold, and the wind blows bioluminescent streamers off waves that collapse beneath their own weight at the surf line. Way down the beach, the lights of Point Loma sparkle sleepily where no one's stirring but maybe a few fire-eyed hipsters or jet-lagged tourists, but even they have sense enough to stay out of the water, which is even darker and colder than the air—particulars appreciated only by sharks. Frankly, the conditions do not seem suitable for sport.

From one of the dim shapes on the beach came a question: "Did that journalist show up? Isn't he supposed to go?"

To participate, I suddenly realized, was to slow these good men down. No way could I keep up with them on a two-mile open ocean night swim. My terror quotient would leach me of adrenaline within a hundred meters and I'd sink like some giant dehydrated apricot. Hampering a training evolution of the U.S. Navy is a deed some Ayatollah-crazed Iranian might relish, but not this Yank. Fidelity to country supersedes fidelity to journalism, and my responsibility was clear. The road to patriotism led down the beach toward breakfast.

O   O   O

SEALs are the progeny of the Underwater Demolition Teams of World War II, which cleared assault beaches before Allied invasions. Today they are trained for infiltration, demolition, reconnaissance, and antiterrorism warfare. Exactly what they do and where they do it is classified, but it is generally conceded by military experts that the SEALs are the toughest unconventional warfare unit on earth—a claim illustrated by the fact that they are among the most decorated combat units in the nation's history.

One rarely hears about the SEALs, and that's generally the way they like it. They have always been a small group (rarely more than 1,200 officers and men) but, in 1983, a Pentagon directive, inspired by escalating terrorism, ordered that the size of the force be increased to 1,800.

"Our retention rate is excellent, about 86 percent—and that includes the loss of retirees," Commander Larry Simmons, executive officer at the Naval Special Warfare Center, told me. "There's a lot of pride among team members, and the life-style is good. SEALs tend to continue on as SEALs, so the only way for us to grow is to make sure good people get into—and *through*—the program."

Which has not been easy. Historically, only 25 to 35 percent of the candidates who enter Basic Underwater Demolition/SEAL (BUD/S) training at Coronado endure the program's intense physical and emotional demands and graduate. Quitting is made diabolically simple: A recruit need only walk into the school's courtyard and ring a brass bell three times, no questions asked. So to meet the Pentagon's muster goals, the Naval Special Warfare Center has not only increased the number of BUD/S classes from five to eight a year, it has also taken a hard look at its training program by commissioning several research projects to inspect techniques, nutrition, and equipment.

"We refuse to make the training easier," Simmons told me, "but we are trying to train smarter. We've increased caloric intake from 3,500 to 5,000 calories a day, and we're pushing carbohydrates in our nutrition briefings. Because we do so much running in jungle boots, tibial stress fractures are a big problem, so now we're trying to develop a boot with a running-shoe sole. In the old days, a trainee was brought in cold and was immediately expected to run 50 miles a week and do intense PT—that's a heck of a physical trauma. The training is designed to eliminate people who don't have the essential mental toughness we require, but losing a good candidate to some common sports injury really hurts. So now, working with experts, we've devised a good basic three-month conditioning program recruits are supposed to follow prior to even getting here. And, once they arrive, they go immediately into Fourth Phase (a seven-week preconditioning course). We're giving them every opportunity to ready themselves for basic BUD/S training. This has cut down on sports injuries, and it's lowered our recidivism rate. But not enough. We still have a lot of work to do."

But, as one BUD/S instructor told me, the attitude of a trainee has as much to do with his success at Coronado as his physical ability. "There's no sure success profile where you can say one type of guy will make it and another won't. Some guys come in looking like Wally Cox, but finish like tigers. The only exceptions are the Rambo types— guys with weight-lifter muscles who want to go out, get fucked up on the weekends, and crack some heads in a bar fight. I've been here a lot of years, and I've yet to see one of those guys make it. For one thing, we don't want chest-beaters and we won't tolerate that kind of attitude. For another, that kind of person lacks the emotional maturity it takes to survive here. Being mean is something quite different from being tough and, if they don't wash out in the first few weeks, they're always gone by the end of Hell Week. The thread that ties almost all the successful trainees is that they are generally very bright and highly motivated. Essentially, I think, they see themselves as athletes."

Hell Week is something one hears much about in Coronado. Five or six weeks into the first of three training stages, SEAL candidates endure what is basically a five-day nonstop triathlon without sleep. Instructors (working 12-hour shifts) keep recruits moving through field training, ocean swims, runs, mud crawls, and obstacle courses 24-hours a day, stopping only to eat.

"If a trainee makes it through Hell Week," Lieutenant Rick May, officer in charge of preconditioning, told me, "you can be fairly sure he's going to make it through the rest of the training, even though the training gets progressively more demanding. When a man makes it into Third Phase (the twenty-fourth week of the program), workouts start getting serious. We do 5½-mile swims, 14-mile runs, and unbelievable PTs. The guys have to do 21 pull-ups before they can go eat a meal. The program tends to extract physical conditioning through natural challenges and obstacles rather than from time lifting weights in a gym—we feel it's more productive. It produces more strength and less bulk. You see these guys after Hell Week, and they're all broken down; not much in the way of muscle definition. But take a look at the guys in Third Phase. They look like Olympic wrestlers."

One trainee, who had recently completed Hell Week, told me, "It was tempting to go ask for the bell." (During Hell Week, instructors carry the brass bell with them.) "Guys kept dropping out. We lost nearly half our group in the first 48 hours. As they left, we'd run in place and sing "Happy Trails to You." It was the only way we had of saying good-bye. When it's 3 a.m. and you're wrestling a damn IBS (inflatable boat) through the surf, freezing your ass off, you come up with plenty of good reasons to quit. I didn't quit but when it was finally over, I broke down and cried—I wasn't the only one, either. A few weeks later, we had this evolution where we do a long night swim through a seal rookery. Definitely great white shark country. Before Hell Week, I would have been terrified. After Hell Week, though, it was like going on a picnic."

○ ○ ○

One might think the difference between a successful aerobics instructor and a more successful BUD/S instructor is the leverage bar of military sadism. In my first few days at Coronado, though, the instructors I observed were less abusive than the average high school football coach and far more positive. ("We're for these guys," May told me. "If they don't succeed, the program doesn't succeed.") Yet, from the trainees, I was hearing how tough the instructors were—never said with anger, but with the sort of dark joy used to impress outsiders. The instructor most often discussed was Bobby Richardson; better known to his students as the Anti-Christ. One morning I arrived on the beach at 5:15 a.m.—slightly late, unfortunately, to participate in a four-mile run (sub seven-minute miles), but just in time to hear Richardson for the first time. A student (an Annapolis graduate, so he had to be called "sir" by the instructors) had also arrived late, so now, at Richardson's request, he was sitting fully clothed in the water.

"What happens when we're late, sir?"

"We get to enjoy the water, Instructor Richardson!"

"Is the water nice, sir?"

"Hoo-YAH, Instructor Richardson."

"Sir, I have had four cups of fucking coffee and I'm like a fucking wild man. Piss me off again and I'll show you why SEAL-fucking training is the roughest military training on planet-fucking Earth. I'll bet you laid around in bed listening to the surf report at the Wedge."

"We're going surfing at the Wedge this weekend, Instructor Richardson."

"AND YOU DIDN'T INVITE ME?"

"I was going to invite you, Instructor Richardson, I really was—"

"Sir, I have personally busted my ass for you, and you don't even invite me to go surfing?"

"I was going to loan you my boogie board—"

"BOOGIE BOARD? That really hurts, sir. Now you've gone and broke my fucking heart."

Richardson, 30, interested me not just because of his command of the language but because it was like meeting Sergeant Vince Carter incarnate, or so I hoped. The guy's about 5'9" and looks like he has been force-fed protein tablets since infancy (with a slingshot, maybe) and seemed a prime candidate to provide me with those colorful, irreverent quotes journalists so love. But that afternoon, riding with Richardson to a local skeet range, he was telling me, "Anybody can be hard. That's easy. What's difficult is to be fair. The students come from such a dichotomy of backgrounds, we have to be tough on them to make them work together. If I play the bad guy, they must necessarily unite; pull together against me. It works."

Dichotomy of backgrounds? Must necessarily unite? Well, this wasn't Vince Carter talking. (Later, Chief Dave Walters, another instructor, would tell me, "Bobby's got the best act in the unit. Even the higher-ups believe it. But the truth is, he's probably the most compassionate instructor we have. When things get too tough on the students, he'll call us aside and say, 'Time to back off.' He's a real leader.") But for the moment, finding the Anti-Christ replaced by an articulate Richardson was a disappointment. Yet it was Richardson who best reduced fitness to its lowest common denominator: "You take one type of person—civilian, military, it doesn't matter—and put him on the most scientifically sound nutrition program, run him through a state-of-the-art training routine with a bunch of high-tech equipment, and he still won't come out in top shape. But take another type of person, stick him barefoot on the beach with a rope to climb and some water to swim in, and he'll come out lean and mean; a real tiger. It's not physical toughness, it's mental toughness. Fitness is a by-product of personal integrity."

The Great Equalizers

ohn Galland has a face made for Pendleton shirts and a body made for canoeing. His arms are the size of legs, and if you are in a boat with him and sluff off for a moment, he might say something like, "You starting to cramp up? You tired? Why don't you just kick back for awhile and let me paddle?"

Which is why I don't like riding in the front of a canoe. Your partner can see too much. Your paddling techniques are open to inspection and every meditative pause invites comment: "Your face is looking a little flushed. Maybe you should drink some water and rest." As a professional outdoors person, I prefer the privacy of the stern, where one may rudder or meditate free of guilt and the frenzied expectations of nonstop paddling.

Fat chance on this trip.

There were eight of us on this four-day journey into southwest Florida's Ten Thousand Islands, a convoluted tidal region of mangrove islands and dark water, much of which is part of Everglades National Park. Because most of the islands look the same, even the simplest of courses demands constant attention and, because the cuts are so narrow, tides run with the velocity of rank rivers. Paddling into those tides is no easy chore even from the stern, and with guys like Galland around, one has to either paddle hard or be humiliated with kindness: "See the nice birds? Why don't you just look at the birds for awhile?"

Galland is a good example of a brand of outdoor enthusiast being seen in increasing numbers in wilderness regions of this country. He is not just good at one sport, he is good at nearly all sports, yet he is so thoughtful and charming it's almost impossible to hate him for it. In the winter, he favors Alpine skiing at Breckenridge, though ice sailing is an option too. In the fall, spring, and summer, he's busy canoeing Minnesota's boundary waters, or scuba diving, or white-water rafting, or sailing or swimming, or maybe surfing in the Bahamas.

"Water," he says, "frozen or otherwise, is the great equalizer."

Yet, on this trip, things didn't seem exactly equal. Of the eight of us in canoes, Galland and just three others had the huge upper bodies necessary for power stroking. But fortunately, only Galland had the paddling experience to convert all that muscle into motion, so there were many rest stops, many water breaks, much hanging onto mangrove limbs while the tide jettisoned passed in fantastic streaks and swirls. Under such circumstances, I could hardly be accused of being the only laggard in the group.

That first day in the Ten Thousand Islands, we made the long backcountry crossing to White Horse Key, a barrier island of palm trees with beaches as bright as packed snow. When our canoes finally touched shore, I sat there sweating, weary, but Galland and his buddies were anxious to get out and explore. No, they didn't need my help. Yes, they would be easy to find. "Just follow our tracks," Galland called to me, as I watched them roll away against the pale green backdrop of the Gulf of Mexico, the aluminum of their four wheelchairs glittering in the winter sunlight.

The Great Equalizers

○ ○ ○

No one knows the exact figures, but it is estimated there are ten million Americans below the age of 65 who have a lower-extremity mobility impairment. And each year, 15,000 more suffer some kind of spinal cord injury and must face the reality that much of their lives will be spent in wheelchairs.

"But not all of their lives," Galland will tell you. "It doesn't work that way anymore."

More than 19 years ago, just three days past his twentieth birthday, Galland skied off a hill in Colorado and hit an aspen tree. Prior to his accident, he had lived what he describes as "a severely able-bodied life." The son of outdoor enthusiasts, he had been skiing, rock climbing, and white-water canoeing since age ten, and the doctors' prognosis—that he would never walk again—was not easily accepted.

"Like everyone else," he says "I went through a denial period. I thought sure I'd have some kind of miraculous healing because there was no way I was meant to be a paraplegic. I was 20-years-old; I was *immortal.* It took me two or three years to finally accept that the doctors were right, and that didn't make it any better. I'd look at a mountain or a river rapid, and I'd think: I'll never be able to do what I used to do again. It was not a happy time. See, one of the problems was that we had no role models back then. You never saw any disabled people on the ski slopes. Or in canoes. Or even on hiking trails in national parks. Back then, people in chairs were invisible; like they were expected to stay inside and watch the soaps."

Galland had his personal awakening after five years in a chair. "I was out in the woods with a friend of mine, Shorty Powers, and we were wheeling around, tipping over, giggling like fools, and that's when it dawned on me: I'm not made out of eggshells. If I tip over, it's okay. *I'm not glued to this chair.*"

Coincidentally, at about the same time, America was going through its own awakening regarding wheelchair athletes and outdoor enthusiasts. The federal government began taking its first slow steps to ensure architectural access to wheelchair users while, from the general population, disabled leaders in outdoor sports began to emerge.

One of the most important leaders, then and now, is Barry Corbett. Corbett, now in his fifties, was one of America's premier mountaineers in the 1960s. He was a member of the 1963 Everest expedition, guided in the Tetons, ran a ski lodge, and was part of the government-assisted expedition that climbed most of the important peaks in Antarctica. But in 1968, while photographing skiers, he was injured in a helicopter crash and, as all spinal cord injury victims must, found himself facing some unsettling realities.

"As far as I know, there were no disabled climbers or skiers at that time," he told me by phone from his home in Englewood, Colorado, "but I knew I wanted to be as active as I could be. So I started kayaking. Kayaking was a great substitute for the things I thought I could no longer do. With kayaking, I could get the same sort of intimate physical involvement I used to get out of climbing."

Corbett kayaked a number of white-water rivers, including the Grand Canyon and the main fork of the Salmon River, though he says, "Not any of them were exceptionally difficult by normal kayaking standards. It's just that no one expected to see a gimp doing them."

In 1980, Corbett published a book, *Options: Spinal Cord Injury and the Future*, which not only articulated his personal feelings about what it's like to be a disabled outdoorsman, but also pointed disabled readers toward a myriad of new horizons. (The book, in its seventh printing, is available free through the National Spinal Cord Injury Association, 600 West Cummings Park, Suite 2000, Woburn, MA 01801.)

Says Galland, "Barry and his book gave a lot of people their lives back. He was probably our first national role model."

After the publication of *Options,* it became increasingly common to see disabled people enjoying sports previously thought accessible only to able-bodied people. Around the country, organizations promoting outdoor sports for the disabled began to gather numbers and strength: groups such as Breckenridge Outdoor Education Center, Snow Bird Adaptive, SPLORE, Cooperative Wilderness Handicapped Outdoor Group (C. W. HOG), Mission Bay Aquatic Sports Center, and others. (For a complete list, write: Spinal Network, P.O. Box 4162, Boulder, CO 80306.)

Says Corbett, "I have no idea what effect my book did or did not have. I do feel that, while many good things happened during the last decade, disabled people also created a sort of trap for themselves. We spent a lot of time proving there was nothing we couldn't do. A team of wheelchair climbers climbed the highest peak in Texas. A team of kayakers paddled around Prince William Sound. Hopefully, disabled people of this decade won't feel pushed by an ethic that is no longer valid—that we have to set records or do everything as well as able-bodied people. People make the mistake of seeking a transference between a sporting event and a life event, and that has never been my point. For instance, to a quadriplegic, a kayak paddle doesn't mean very much."

Galland, who has become one of this country's most dynamic spokespeople for the disabled-in-the-outdoors movement, says the point is that now, at least, there are options. "No one expects to end up in a wheelchair. No one even thinks about it, let alone *plans* on it. But when it happens, an outdoor experience is the best way I know for a person to learn that he's not wheelchair bound. A wheelchair is just one of a number of options, which now include kayaks or sailboats or climbing ropes or Arroya skis."

O O O

The option of choice on this trip is canoes. Eight men, four canoes—each loaded with food, camping gear, and a wheelchair for our visits ashore. The trip was organized by North Carolina Outward

Bound, one of a growing number of organizations that recognize the validity of outdoor experiences for all people. Our route through the Ten Thousand Islands may be complex, but our routine is simple: We paddle during the day, then make camp on one of the sandy barrier islands before sunset. Galland and veteran Outward Bound instructor Matt West are in charge but, happily, they let us set our own pace.

The pace we set is not slow, but after the demands of that first day, it is not exactly frantic either. We spend a lot of time talking around camp fires, the disabled guys sitting in chairs, the rest of us in sand. Over the course of a few days, everyone tells his story. Galland describes his confrontation with the aspen tree. Paul Stempel of San Diego was injured in Vietnam. Bill Palmer of Lemon Grove, California, tells of his skydiving accident just over two years ago. Andy Fleming, director of sports and recreation for the Paralyzed Veterans of America, recounts how, at age 24, he tried to crawl under a train at precisely the wrong time. Mostly, though, they talk about what they're doing now. We spend a lot of time laughing, and considerations of how we sit or where we sit are rendered inconsequential by the strength of the personalities involved.

Later, Fleming, whose organization represents 14,000 disabled Americans, would tell me, "Good things have happened for disabled people in this country. But there's still more to do. Access is still a big problem. We don't want wilderness areas paved. But if paths are going to be established for the general public, we feel the extra steps should be taken to make them wide enough for wheelchairs. And a rating system for wilderness areas like the kind they use to rate the difficulty of river rapids would help too." (According to a spokesman at the National Park Service, a 1–5 rating system for the disabled will soon be in use.)

"Basically," says Fleming, "we just want to be a part of the mainstream. When I was first injured, I had to deal with my own prejudice against disabled people. I didn't want to associate with them because I didn't see myself as one of them. But then I finally realized what more and more able-bodied people are beginning to realize: We're all just people, and our abilities and our interests vary. In the outdoors, some of us can keep up and some of us can't."

Fleming was right. After the first day, I kept up just fine.

The Outward Bound

Mutiny

—

*T*UESDAY (BASE CAMP, BIG PINE KEY)   The opening day of
Outward Bound's first sea school in the Florida Keys. I arrived this morning expecting instructors who believe that
hardship borders on hilarity, and figuring, also, that if things get too
ecstatic I might just mosey on down to Key West alone, where I have
often thought a man could make a decent living renting seeing-eye
dogs to drunks.

But so far it's easy; nothing even as demanding as, say, Hell Week
at a midwestern Bible college. There are about 20 of us—adults from
Maine, Connecticut, Texas, Pennsylvania, Georgia, and sundry other
places—who have paid $525 each for this two-week Outward Bound
Experience. I am one of three from Florida, and one of two who have
not been through an Outward Bound course before. But students and
instructors are going out of their way to keep me from feeling like an
outsider, steering me into their well-loved stories of hardship in America's six Outward Bound schools. I see already that I will like the people here. I am less certain about the course itself.

Batfishing in the Rainforest

I came fearing a 14-day Paradise Island encounter for businessmen and wealthy Ivy Leaguers, individuals in search of—you know—an *adventure*. Instead, this first day more resembled a mini-jamboree à la Boy Scouts U.S.A. We jogged about a mile, swam all of 80 yards, and then plowed our way through two marathon meetings. The swimming and running I don't mind. The meetings drive me crazy. Suddenly I find I am number eight of Spoonbill Watch (the other group is Osprey Watch). When our instructor yells "Count off!" our group replies, "One!" "Two!" "Three!" "Four!" "Five!" "Six!" "Seven!" And then I hear myself go—"Eight?" I haven't been a number or a species of bird since fourth-grade reading class, when I was a Redbird. Fast readers, the creeps, were Bluebirds.

O O O

WEDNESDAY (BASE CAMP) More meetings. In the most recent, we discussed our upcoming trip. We will take two 30-foot spritsail pulling (row) boats from the Lower Keys across Florida Bay to the Everglades, up the Shark River on Florida's west coast, around Cape Sable, where we are to "solo" (two days alone on the beach), and then back to the Keys—a trip of about 200 miles in all. We were also informed that the process of body-waste elimination would be a matter of hanging the necessary equipment over the side and relaxing. One of my fellow students, Jim Rojek, who already has been nicknamed "Zonker" (as in Doonesbury) because of his long hair, goatee, and late-sixties vocabulary, seemed especially upset at this news and took me aside to confide, "It's like, since I was *ten,* man, I haven't sat on a stool without a sports section in my hands."

I was content to leave my own reservations unspoken, and we discussed Euell Gibbons, with Zonker concluding, finally, that he was not only a very heavy dude but probably could have played major league baseball if properly motivated as a child.

The Outward Bound Mutiny

O   O   O

THURSDAY (UNDER WAY, BOUND FOR CONCH KEY OFF MARATHON)
Aboard this open 30-foot boat we have a Texas hippie, a born-again
Christian, a lawyer disguised as a district-court-of-appeals judge, a
Canadian, a Princeton Tiger, a former parakeet trainer, a guy who
once considered monkhood in Nepal, a former male model, a topogra-
pher, and me. Normally, with individuals as diverse as these stuck in
cramped quarters and fed on bulghur, vegetables, and no beer at all, I
would have expected shipmates to start dying quite suddenly while being stabbed or choked. But my instructors and fellow students are unusual people—likable, interesting, and obviously aware of what two
weeks on a small boat can do to one's affection for mankind. At night
we sleep on a mattress of oars and giggle about our discomfort like
kids at a slumber party. During the days we talk, wait on meals, row
when it is necessary, then talk some more. Our assistant watch officer
can juggle, the judge could have been a stand-up comedian, and the
former parakeet trainer can sing. Hire Mickey Rooney and we could
take this show to Broadway.

Even so, I find myself becoming increasingly dissatisfied with the
Outward Bound Experience. Nothing so dramatic as being completely
pissed off, but unhappy enough to consider jumping ship tomorrow
morning when we pass beneath the bridge at Marathon. I *wanted* to like
Outward Bound. I really did. Ever since I was 14 or 15 and read about
the Hurricane Island, Maine, course in *Reader's Digest,* I've wanted to
see what it was like. Here were kids a little older than I jumping off
cliffs, running until they dropped, and having no end of good times,
while, a thousand miles and three or four hundred dollars away, the
pinnacle of my day's excitement was killing barn rats with a Louisville
Slugger and riding hogs.

So now I am 27. And, at first glance, the Outward Bound philosophy is still attractive. It's called "experiential education"—a struc-

tured, deliberate learning process that uses challenges found in natural settings as a teaching medium. Through courses in mountain climbing, sea survival, white-water canoeing, and the like, Outward Bound's goal (in spite of the brochure hype that peddles "oneness with self and nature") seems to be putting modern men and women back in touch with things increasingly alien: their physical and mental strengths and weaknesses—and, more to the point, their humanity.

And Americans have accepted it with open arms. When the first American Outward Bound school opened in Colorado in 1962 it was a sort of rites-of-manhood program for about 100 teenage boys. Today there are schools in Colorado, New Mexico, North Carolina, Minnesota, Oregon, Maine (with which the Florida school is associated), and a center at Dartmouth College. Every year, more than 6,000 Americans—most of them adults—pay from $200 to $750 to attend Outward Bound courses. The philosophy has become so widely accepted that more than 300 high schools and colleges offer experiential-education courses, and there are a growing number of Outward Bound–type schools around, such as the popular National Outdoor Leadership School based in Lander, Wyoming.

It's all very neat. Very healthy. And very promotable: *Americans Turn Again to the Wilderness in Search of Themselves!* It's marquee stuff.

But I don't like it. Somehow, it grates on me. Outward Bound has turned hardship into a very nifty little commodity—it's sort of the McDonald's of adversity, peddling a strange brewing of moral Metrecal and military discipline. The organization brings systemization, of all things, to the wilderness. And as Outward Bound's liability insurance rates climb higher and higher, the more systemized the program will get. In 15 years of operation, the six schools have "lost" (a spokeswoman's term) ten participants—the result being that I now sit here in this boat clutching a life jacket while the lovely wilderness world of the Florida Keys drifts by.

But Outward Bound is still popular. And it will always be popular.

The Outward Bound Mutiny

Experiential-education schools cater to America's love of packaged goods.

○ ○ ○

FRIDAY (UNDER WAY, HEADING ACROSS FLORIDA BAY)   I tried to jump ship this morning. The bridge off Conch Key and the open road held all the allure of a lovely woman. I told Alan Sterman, our watch officer, that I wanted off. I tried to make it as businesslike and friendly as possible, explaining that I found the course somewhat frustrating, since I wasn't allowed to bring my fishing pole or my snorkel gear, and that I thought it best for all if I just headed on home to my boat and my dogs. Immediately, he called a meeting of the watch and, for an hour, they talked to me like a brother, extolling the virtues of the Outward Bound Experience. They are intelligent, sincere people, and, as a result, I have begun to doubt my own instincts. Maybe I've been wrong all along. I've decided to stay and see.

○ ○ ○

SATURDAY (UNDER WAY, BOUND FOR FLAMINGO AT THE BASE OF THE FLORIDA PENINSULA)   Everybody gets to be token captain at least once on this two-week excursion, and today is my day. I say "token" captain because it is difficult to give commands when you can't differentiate between, say, a mizzen and a sprit.

However, being no rookie when it comes to wading into uncharted intellectual waters, I am going at it with enthusiasm. Already we have gone aground four times, and I have further adventures in sight. Bruce Dyleski, my Texas buddy-system partner, is my navigator. Together we seem to have an unfailing nose for calamity. Our methods are simple: Bruce uses the charts to locate oyster bars, shallow water, old pilings, and other points of interest, and then I use the tiller to aim for them. Outward Bound's whole philosophy is based on learning through trying, physical experiences, and thus far my crew has had the good fortune to experience what it is like to push a four-ton boat out of water a foot deep. Under my firm leadership, I sense that the crew has never before been so united, so affirmed in a common goal. To a man, it is talking mutiny. One more collision and I fear civil war.

○ ○ ○

SATURDAY (AFTERNOON)   My irritation at not being able to fish the whole trip was inflamed again when, while rowing past the marina at Flamingo, a fishing-guide friend of mine, Captain John Scudder, recognized me and yelled, "Hey boy! What're you doing on that thing—the snook are hitting!"

Irritation turned immediately to melancholy. I pointed to our rowers and yelled back, "I bought all four of these guys in Taiwan—deal was too good to pass up!"

Laughing derisively at our Viking-style boats, he turned and walked away. Now I know how tourists feel on the Key West "Conch Train."

○ ○ ○

SUNDAY (MORNING)   Up the Shark River, flushing spoonbills, egrets, and herons as we go. The mangroves tower above this dark river, and we proceed in unctuous quiet. During his sunrise urination, our watch officer, Alan Sterman, looked out upon this tapestry of water and jungle, yawned, and observed, "Ah, well, well. Another shitty day in paradise."

○ ○ ○

SUNDAY (AFTERNOON)   I am riding aboard our convoy mate, boat number 1, for a few hours so that I can get to know the other watch officers and students. The mood here is drastically different from what I am used to. Our boat thrives on jokes, good humor, juggling contests, and benevolent lies. This boat feeds on rules and thrives on discipline.

Zonker is a member of boat number 1, and he's having a pretty tough time of it. And I can undestand why. A few minutes ago I took out a pack of Red Man tobacco to have a comforting chew. Immediately, I was informed that Outward Bounders are not allowed to use tobacco. I can understand rules against smoking—smoking is an offensive and deadly habit. But chewing? Chewing is harmless—if the person involved has any sort of aim at all. But not wishing to upset what harmony there is on this boat, I put my Red Man away and, on the sly, took a pinch from a tin of snuff. No one was watching but Zonker. Immediately, he was at my side asking what I had just taken.

"Skoal," I whispered back. "It's great. Want to try some?"

He did. And when the pinch of tobacco had been deposited between his lip and gum, Zonker moved away, intent on savoring this new drug in solitude. But in a few minutes he was back, whispering again, "Hey, man—gettin' a pretty nice buzz off this stuff. Yeah, kind of a warm sort of rush."

He's sitting in the stern now, but every time our eyes meet, he winks and gives me the O.K. sign with his hand. I'm going to have a hard time making him believe that Skoal doesn't come to the U.S. via midnight boats from Campeche.

○ ○ ○

TUESDAY (ON THE BEACH AT CAPE SABLE)   As I write this, I sit alone on a desolate sweep of beach, hell-bent on forging a lofty thought or two. It is the seventh day of Outward Bound's first Florida sea school, and I am on solo—abandoned here to wrestle around with metaphysics and parley with the cosmos while stoking my physical fires on a grand total of two carrots, two oranges, and a gallon of water.

Outward Bound is bullish on metaphysics. Before the boat dropped us off, our instructors braced us for the ordeal with three consecutive inspirational readings and a few moments of silence. During the silence, Zonker winked at me and proffered another O.K. sign. One more hit of Skoal, and he'll be trading one-liners with God.

So I am alone. Well, not completely alone. I have pitched my tarp over a driftwood stump, and a few dozen ants are marching up my leg, merry as Nazis. I feel a metaphysical reverie coming on, tempered by my respect for fire ants. Noting their expert rank and file—and the million years of evolution and practice thus implied—I took out my official Outward Bound notebook and made my first entry: "If practice were the only criterion for human expertise, we would all be qualified urologists."

Profound.

My instructors will be proud.

O O O

TUESDAY (ON SOLO)   Second entry in my official Outward Bound notebook: "Life and Outward Bound have much in common—the people are nice, but the circumstances are pretty much a pain in the ass."

O O O

WEDNESDAY (BOUND FOR THE KEYS, ACROSS FLORIDA BAY)   Night sailing; running with the speed of the nocturnal clouds. A windblown night, with bioluminescence feathering the breaking waves and throwing a wake of green fire behind the boat. We lay upon our bed of oars, joking and laughing softly. All is darkness but for the reluctant stars and a few dim lights on the horizon. I am forever curious about such lights—the lights that mark the nocturnal strongholds of human existence in all desolate or rural places—and I pass the night away in speculation, admiring them all, wishing them luck, one by one by one.

O O O

THURSDAY (UNDER WAY)   Becalmed. In the fresh head of midday, islands shimmering in the far distance take on the qualities of a mirage. The crew's sense of community feeds on this idle time, and conversations pioneer fresh and interesting territory: flying saucers, the future of the Beatles, mysticism, God, the value of urine in treating bee stings, and differences in the various Outward Bound schools. The consensus is that the other courses are much tougher—physically and mentally—than this Florida excursion. I believe it. I think I've gained at least five pounds.

○ ○ ○

THURSDAY (EVENING, AT ANCHOR) Our Outward Bound Experience seems to vacillate between the maddening and contrived adventures of Boy Scouts of America and the real dramatics only nature can provide. Unfortunately, it's been long on contrivance and short on experiences that transpire naturally and, therefore, are genuine. This afternoon we sailed past the Content Keys, which afford some of the best fishing and diving anywhere, and the frustration I have felt this whole trip was magnified by the numerous coral heads we floated over—but did not explore—and the simple presence of the vast and empty clear-water flats with their stock of permit, bonefish, and barracuda. We visit many places, but rarely encounter anything. I talked this evening with Dana Chalfant, a sensitive guy who left college for world travel and now runs a landscaping service in Pennsylvania, and he pointed out that I obviously have to see the course differently from others because I live in Florida and spend a lot of time on the water.

"But for me," he added, "a Florida Outward Bound course is one of the few ways to shed society and all of its tourist-oriented trappings."

He is right, of course. We all process our encounters through different channels of likes and dislikes, through myriad layers of experiences and prejudices as varied as our own varied backgrounds. I realize that some of the limitations I have put on this program are tainted with my own limitations—but honesty is all any of us really has to contribute. And I honestly think I would have loved Outward Bound—when I was 16.

○ ○ ○

FRIDAY (UNDER WAY) It is near sunset, and we are sailing into Key West, bound, like so many crews before us, for a brief shore call there. The tide is running hard as we sail toward Mallory Docks, upon which the daily cast of freaks and drifters, tourists and dopeheads stands listening to the conga drummers play and the street merchants hawk their wares. There is a carnival atmosphere, an air of theatrics stagelighted by the sun as it vaporizes on the turquoise horizon. And, we realize now, we are vying for center ring in our Viking-style pulling boats.

Behind me, a crew member cheers nervously, "Let's go in there and show them what Outward Bound is all about!"

Our honor newly fired, with esprit de corps on almost every face, we turn landward and immediately ram bow-first into a tripod of pilings and, caught in the foul tide, drift dangerously backward, our newly broken tiller fluttering like an injured wing.

There is minor chaos before we mount a steering oar, while, from the docks, the freaks and dopeheads jeer, their dull eyes glowing. Finally, our two watch officers secure us to the dock with the calm of experts—which they are—and begin a short lecture on how we, as Outward Bound students, should conduct ourselves while visiting Key West.

But my decision has been made. I hug my friends good-bye, inform the instructors that I am jumping ship, and exchange warm farewells with them, too.

As I hoist my duffel bag up onto the docks, an assistant watch officer from our sister ship asks invectively, "Just where do you think you're going?"

I tell him, "First I'm going to eat some fish at the El Cacique, then call a friend at the sheriff's department, and get a ride to my car—it's that simple."

"How about a few reasons why?" he insists.

"How's this?" I reply. "I'm 27 years old and I want to leave."

And I did.

Authors Note: Through a strange series of coincidences,—too bizarre to detail—my association with Outward Bound has continued over the years. I realize now that I should have taken the course for different reasons, and in a different environment. Outward Bound has been a hugely valuable experience for tens of thousands. Innovative business administrators now regularly send employees through the course—administrators who would have hired neither Zonker or me, and for good reason.

The Best Tarpon
Fisherman in Singapore

*W*hen traveling beyond Singapore with a guy like Alvin Lim Teck, it is only prudent to have an alibi rigged and ready just in case the law swoops down and begins asking uncomfortable questions. Questions like: Did you know this is private property? Where is your fishing license? Why did you choose to travel with this Chinese dope fiend?

Such questions are not asked gently in Singapore or Malaysia, and it's best to be prepared; have the explanation memorized in advance. Be ready to hammer the answers right back with a CIA swagger: Who the hell are *you* to be questioning *me*? Attitude counts for a lot here, but a convincing delivery is not easy when you know that, if convicted of the first two offenses, the authorities will strip you bare and beat you with a rotan stick, probably in front of a crowd of hooting sampan women. If convicted of the latter offense, they will march you off to dung central, then hang you. It doesn't matter that you are an American; doesn't matter that you are a working journalist, travel-addled from four weeks on the road; doesn't matter that you have never even gotten a speeding ticket, let alone aspired to drug trafficking. They will shove you up the steps, put a rope around your neck, and pull the lever. That quick, you can go from innocent journalist searching for a fish to part of the Penang food chain, making a lot of skinny dogs happy.

Don't count on guys like Alvin Lim Teck for help. Alvin the Chinese dope fiend.

O O O

Even if you meet Alvin, you can't help but like Singapore. Singapore is bright, clean, safe; one of those cities that seems to create its own breezes. Downtown, you can send a fax, buy raw ginseng root, invest in a mutual fund, or select a live snake for lunch. Options can be constructed to satisfy any need and arranged to fit any mood. The most famous reminder of Singapore's colonial days is Raffles Hotel, opened in 1887, a great white museum of a place with high ceilings, hardwood floors, palm gardens, and enough elegance in its old walls to overcome the impression that the hotel has been reduced to a parody of its own history. Raffles Hotel does have some history. Joseph Conrad may have roomed here. Rudyard Kipling, Hermann Hesse, and Somerset Maugham did—and wrote about it. In 1902, the island's last tiger was supposedly shot and killed in the hotel billiard room. In 1915 a hotel barman created the Singapore Gin Sling, which is what British colonials spent the evening drinking on 14 February 1942 in defiance of the invading Japanese—who took Singapore the next day. The Japanese appropriated Raffles as officer housing, slaughtered a lot of people, then took time to rename the inn *Syonan Ryokan,* which means "light of the south hotel."

You may be able to resist such places. I can't. They draw me like a magnet—despite the hokey rickshaw rides out front and the Jaga doorman in his white pith helmet. It's like walking into a time capsule, only better because time capsules don't serve buffet breakfast in a garden wild with Asiatic songbirds, nor do they have bars with a faded sign posted: *This Establishment Recommended for Her Majesty's Forces.*

It was while in the Raffles bar that I met tiny, smiling, Ho Wee How, Somerset Maugham's houseboy for many years. ("I didn't even known Mr. Maugham was famous until after he died. He wrote every morning in the garden, then drank whiskey.") Ho Wee How is now the hotel's bar captain, and during our conversation I mentioned to him that, while in Singapore, I wanted to visit the wholesale fish markets. I was looking for a fish.

"A fish? You have lost a fish?"

No, but there was a fish I wanted to find. When I travel, I always carry a photograph of a tarpon because looking for tarpon is a hobby of mine. The tarpon is a popular game fish (in appearance, a giant herring), but its life history is not well-known. It is generally considered a warm-water, saltwater species, but the ocean has no fences, and this photo had once led me to a man in Ireland who swore he caught one ("I decided to kill the beast and study it") and to a population of immature or stunted fish trapped in a Guatemalan lake a hundred miles from the nearest sea. Popular literature says that the Asiatic species, the oxeye tarpon (one of only two species worldwide), is an important food fish, but I had carried this photograph long enough to know that popular literature is sometimes wrong. Ho Wee How was enthusiastic. He led me to Raffles's front entrance and spoke to the Jaga in fast Hainanese. The Jaga straightened his pith helmet and told the cabdriver: "Take this gentleman where he can see a fish!"

The place to see fish on this island is the Teka Market in north Singapore, a great open warehouse of buying and selling where sea creatures from all Asia flop in baskets or lie glassy-eyed on ice. I saw stingrays and skates, varieties of shrimps, lobster, unfamiliar sharks, mackerel, chunks of tunas and swordfish cut in big sections like cheeses, and whole bins filled with live snails and blue crabs. But no tarpon, not one. A withered man studied my photograph while he used a bullock horn to cleave through some kind of grouper. He spoke no English, but he seemed to indicate he knew where I might be able to get information on this fish, and showed me a card, which I copied: *SIOW HONG LONG, Beach Road, All Kinds of Fishing Tackles, Chinese and Japanese Fishing Nets.*

So I took a cab to Singapore's Chinatown and found Siow Hong Long, a cluttered shop of creosoted rope and boxes of long-line gear. It was here I met Alvin Lim Teck, a Chinese man about my own age, shopping for tackle. Alvin said he recognized the fish in my photograph. He said he would take me to catch a tarpon, if I would buy him a reel. I said I might do that—but *after* I saw the fish. Alvin said that was okay too. Alvin told me he was the best tarpon fisherman in all Singapore; it was not a gambling matter.

O O O

Alvin speaks in a rapid, chuckling combination of Chinese, Malay, and English; a verbal stream-of-consciousness that would be numbing if the guy wasn't so funny. It's as if his hands are connected to his jaw; everything moving at once, like an Oriental Barney Fife on some very serious speed.

We ride squashed together in the front seat of a tiny truck, with Alvin's friend, Chiang Loy, at the wheel. At least, Alvin says Chiang Loy is his friend, but I am not so sure, judging from Chiang Loy's heated replies to Alvin's constant criticism of his slow driving: "Fock you, Aw-rin! Fock you!"

Singapore's laws are strict—jaywalking, an immediate $50 fine; littering, an immediate $100 fine; and many cars are rigged with orange roof lights that flash if their drivers exceed the speed limit. Chiang Loy's truck has no flashing light, but the man is no fool. There are black and white Nissan police cars everywhere, and we make our way slowly north on the Bukit Timah Road as Alvin yells to me, "This road take you all the way to London, except we plobably get blowed up in Iraq. Hey Chiang, you take us to London?"

"Fock you, Aw-rin!"

The Best Tarpon Fisherman in Singapore

Outside the city of Singapore, the countryside brightens to Day-Glo green; an extraordinary green that seems to absorb the sun. Forests of exotic hardwoods and hills of palm, curry, and mango incandesce with internal energy: blue-greens, black-greens, gold-greens so radiant that it is as if the earth is the true source of light, the sun only a bright mirror. Chiang begins to take back roads, his truck throwing a dust wake as water buffalo look on, mildly interested. It seems to me we are getting farther and farther from the sea, but I long ago stopped trusting my own bad sense of direction. We cross a wooden bridge, then another. Good God, I wonder, have we crossed illegally into Malaysia? I ask Alvin, who replies at length, but all I understand is that we need to get some rivers.

Rivers?

"Yes," he says. "Bait. Thailand chicken rivers—they ver-ly good bait."

Ah, *livers*. Of course.

By now we have entered a rural settlement. Brown children scatter toward their mothers, laughing, while chickens forage in the sand. One of the shacks displays a rusting *Join the Pepsi Generation* sign, and Alvin signals Chiang to stop. Alvin and I get out as Chiang carefully places my fishing gear in the yard, gets back into the truck, and drives away without so much as a farewell fock you, Aw-rin.

Alvin quickly explains that Chiang doesn't like to fish, and that we will have to find another ride back to town. But we're not going to hitchhike, I insist—hitchhiking is illegal. Don't they whack you with a bamboo pole if you're caught hitchhiking? Alvin says he can find us a ride, but it doesn't matter because I'm European. Being European still counts for something in this country, he says. He has told me this before ("Europeans don't need a fishing ricense!") and seems indifferent to my growing doubts about his motives and deaf to my flat claim that I'm not from Europe. At the house, I pay the man for what Alvin says is a bag of Thai chicken livers, then we hike another mile down the road before cutting cross-country through head-high grass.

I lead the way for several hundred yards, bulling blindly along before Alvin says, "You like the animals—maybe see a coabla, huh?"

"Coabla? What's a coabla . . . ? Geezus—" I stop immediately. "*Cobra*. I don't want to see a cobra; you think I want to see a cobra? This is your country, you go first."

"I have already seen them. Ver-ly pretty snakes. 'Sides, you must be first in case someone sees us. They ask, 'Why you trespassing?' You say you lost, Alvin come to find me. They see you European, it be okay."

Alvin correctly interprets the expression on my face and adds quickly: "We almost to the water. You see the tarpons, you not mad anymore, huh?"

"The water" is a big freshwater lake studded with stumps and hedged by cattails and tall grass. Surprisingly, we are not the only ones here. Three men, all Chinese, fix flat stares on me as I burst into their clearing, then visibly relax when Alvin follows a minute later. Alvin holds up the sack of Thai chicken livers as if it were a trophy, and hollers to them in Chinese. While they talk, I piece together my pack rod and tie on a small white bucktail lure (I draw the line at poultry organs for bait) and move off alone to cast. I can't see them, but I can hear Alvin and the men talking through the grass.

After fishing for about 15 minutes without a strike, I feel my lure snag a stump, but then the stump begins to move, and I realize it's not a stump at all, but a fish. It's a fish, and it's taking out line. I yell through the grass to Alvin, watching the water all the while, expecting to see the fish jump—tarpon almost always jump—but it doesn't, and soon I am bending over a strange-looking iridescent green fish with huge scales and a black mouth, about 15 pounds.

"A tioman!" I hear Alvin say, and I look up to see him and his three friends standing over me. They appear interested—even surprised that I have caught something—but mostly what I notice is that all four of them are smoking big, fresh doobies; they are marijuana addicts, each and every one. "That's what you call tarpons," says Alvin, blowing smoke. "We call it tioman."

Well, this fish isn't a tarpon. It looks more like a prehistoric bowfin.

But it is not the time to argue because I have finally figured out what's going on. Alvin has used me as a shield, probably for some minor dope purchase. He's gotten me lost, I'm trespassing, fishing illegally, and now consorting with a bunch of Chinese hippies. If the cops catch us, I figure I deserve to be beaten with sticks, just for being so dumb.

Your honor, as God as my witness, I thought I was buying chicken livers from Thailand....

I don't want to be hanged, nor do I want to show fear—Alvin and this surly pack will leap upon me like wolves. If they will smoke marijuana in Malaysia—or even Singapore—they are capable of any outrage.

I say easily, "Nice looking tarpon, huh, Alvin?" and release the fish, playing it cool.

I endure another hour, then we are finally back on the road. We walk and walk, with Alvin holding out his thumb to the occasional passing truck. Behind us, I hear a vehicle slow, then stop. I look up to see two men in uniform getting out of a black and white Nissan police car.

Christ, this is it.

Alvin, still with the manic grin on his face, begins to talk, but I've had enough. I stride toward the uniforms and interrupt, confessing in a rush, "I'm not from Europe—I was born in *Ohio,* for God's sake!"

The two policemen seem amused.

What the hell do they want from me? It's true that I have been traveling for four weeks and I'm a little weary, and it's true that I'm not sure if I'm in Singapore or Malaysia, but I am still rational; I'm willing to deal. Alvin, who has never stopped talking, continues to talk, and I consider interrupting once more. Maybe offer the cops a frank proposition: Allow me to borrow one of those nasty little Walthers holstered on their hips, and I will shoot Alvin myself. Not kill him, but wing the son-of-a-bitch. He's healthy. He could survive a clean shot to the head, then I could plead guilty to the lesser charge of attempted murder and recruit Chiang Loy as a character witness.

Fock you, Aw-rin!

One of the policeman turns to me and says, "You need a ride back into Singapore?"

"Yes!"

"You're staying at Raffles?"

"Oh, yes!"

With us safely in the back of the car, the policeman continues, "Did you know the Singapore Sling was invented at Raffles? I highly recommend you try one. It's very cool in the Long Bar."

Which is where I presented Alvin with his new reel.

ON THE
ROAD

Curse of the Artifact

Hunters

My friend Bayardo runs a cattle ranch on the Pacific Coast of Costa Rica, and I think he called because he felt my last visit there was not a successful one, what with the broken generator, the dead cook, and the peasant woman who ran screaming into the night.

"This time it will be better," he told me on the telephone. "I have something new for us to try. Looking for *huacas*."

"*Huacas?*"

"Yes, beautiful *huacas* made of hah-day. Up on the hillside that overlooks the bay. It is a short ride on horseback. It will make amends, perhaps, for that distressing night."

I had no idea what *huacas* made of "hah-day" were, or why Bayardo felt obligated to make amends. We had shared a distressing night, true, but it certainly was not his fault—though, like so many Costa Ricans, he tends to blame himself for any small thing that goes wrong.

Batfishing in the Rainforest

Slightly more than a year ago, I had been sitting on the porch of his ranch house, reading by lantern light (the generator was out), which I enjoyed, for the lantern attracted moths and bats more surely than electric bulbs, and it is a pleasant thing to sit with jungle on all sides and watch animals flutter in and out of the darkness. But then I heard a scream that was not pleasant; a primal wail that brought me to my feet, heart pounding, and I ran along the porch toward the back of the house to find Bayardo and several of his workers trying to comfort a maid who was sobbing, hysterical. Finally, she shook free of them and bolted into the woods, waving her arms and still screaming.

Bayardo shrugged sheepishly and nodded toward the door of one of the worker's shacks. "The cook is sick," he said. "She is concerned."

Sick? The cook was a German name Bern, and he had beaten me at chess only the night before. How sick could he be?

"Oh, he is sick more or less," said Bayardo, trying to block my path to the door of the shack.

Did he need a doctor?

"No, I think that is not necessary."

Medicine?

"It is a thing we can ask in the morning, perhaps."

I could see Bern through the open door now. There was an oil lamp by the door—the maid had probably lighted it—and he was lying face down, eyes open, hands like claws. Even on his best days, Bern wasn't what you would call handsome. Now he looked grotesque, and he didn't appear to be breathing.

"He doesn't look sick, Bayardo, he looks dead."

Averting his eyes, Bayardo said, "That is a possibility."

"Don't you think someone ought to check?"

He was suddenly embarrassed, and that's when I realized that neither Bayardo nor anyone else was going into that room at night, especially with the generator broken. I put the oil lamp on the little nightstand, grabbed Bern by the wrists, and flipped him over. He was still warm, but there was no pulse, no respiration. Behind me, Bayardo, his head poked cautiously through the door, was saying, "These peasants, these stupid peasants, they are frightened of death—as if it might crawl up their arms, into their hearts. They will fix their own breakfasts in the morning! And just what they deserve, refusing to touch a man on his deathbed."

That began a long night of searching the woods for the hysterical maid, of trying to calm her, of contacting the medical examiner by radio telephone, of waiting for the small plane to land in the pasture at daylight, of trying to force the by-then uncooperative Bern into the plane's lone passenger seat, of watching the plane bank away over the Pacific—a sight extraordinary for the open window Bern had required and his frozen, cavalier wave.

Which is why Bayardo had called to make amends, inviting me back to the ranch to search for *huacas* made of hah-day on the hillside above the bay, a short horseback ride from the ranch.

"Hah-day," said Bayardo in explanation, "spelled j-a-d-e."

Jade, the gemstone?

"Yes. We burned the hillside last year for pasture and, after the burn, we began to find these things. Strange carvings. Chairs of stone. Indio things, such as the Maya made, though no one knew because of the jungle. Someone took a shovel to the hill and scraped the dirt away in a few places. This person found many small figurines of jade, *huacas*, carvings of animals and people and gods."

Why hadn't he told me this last year, when I was there?

"It was a thing with these stupid peasants," Bayardo explained, "a thing about the hillside being a bad place. They are not like us. They are superstitious fools."

○ ○ ○

Several weeks later, I arrived at the ranch, but it was two or three more days before Bayardo decided he wouldn't have time to take me to the hillside. Instead, he assigned me Jesus, the yardman who, despite a crippled right hand, had once climbed a tree to catch an iguana for my young son and endeared himself to me. Jesus filled two rum bottles with well water, saddled the horses, and we rode deserted beach for more than a mile before cutting inland through pastureland, past cattle drowsing in the shade of gigantic guancaste trees; then the pasture began to ascend toward the mountain forest, at the edge of which we finally stopped, tying our horses.

"It is there," Jesus said, pointing to an eroded slash-and-burn scar a half a mile away and straight up, it seemed. We began to climb, Jesus leading the way with his machete, me trailing behind in the heat, the sound of my own breathing louder than that wild clatter of parrots and the boom of howler monkeys from the forest canopy beyond. I was looking only for footholds on the steep incline, not artifacts, for I knew that Bayardo, in his eagerness to please, sometimes exaggerated. But then I began to see chunks of pottery shard at my feet, then half of a weathered vase—Jesus had walked right over it—and then a three-pedestalled stone seat of a type called *metates* by Latinos. I held it up for Jesus to see, but he only shrugged. "It is nothing," he said. "They are everywhere."

The *metates* were not everywhere, but they were common. At the top of the hill, I stopped and looked down. The hill connected with two other rises to form a sort of amphitheater above the sea, and the entire slope was littered with artifacts: large pottery shards, broken shell tools, and stone chairs; remnants that implied a swarming activity on the now still hillside—an eerie thing, for it was as if the hill had given way without warning, scattering the village and swallowing its builders.

"Let's try here," said Jesus. He was on his knees in one of the erosion scars, and he began to cut slices of earth away with his machete as one might cut cheese. Only a few inches in, the blade nicked something hard, and he used his fingers to extract a small dark stone. He cleaned it on his T-shirt and handed it to me. It was a jade figurine, augured at the top for a necklace, with carved owl's eyes and folded arms. It was a beautiful little thing, cool to the touch, a sentient green being fresh from the earth.

"Hah-day," said Jesus. "Mayan."

I had done enough research prior to my arrival to know that the amulet wasn't actually jade—it was jadeite—and it probably wasn't Mayan, though it could have been. The indigenous people who had once lived on this hillside were probably Chorotegas, the southern-most residents of highly advanced meso-America, a region of civilization that produced a complex system of arithmetic 2,000 years before mathematics came into general use in Europe, and that invented and employed a calendar system more accurate than our own. In the years between 800 and 1200 A.D., the Chorotegas became the region's most prolific producers of carved jade, using it in trade with the Maya to the north and the Inca to the south. I now held one of those jade pieces in my hand.

Jesus scraped for a while longer and found six more amulets, one of soft green stone, another a beautifully carved monkey's face of bright blue jadeite. Then he held the machete out to me. Did I want to try? I'm not going to sit here and lie to you. I wanted to dig—and I did dig, but I did so knowing that I was participating in what has become a national tragedy. As Ricardo Lopez Quesada, a San José attorney and author of *Costa Rica: The Southern Frontier of Meso-America,* told me by phone before my arrival, "All over Costa Rica there are thousands of unexcavated sites such as the one your friend has discovered. He may legally keep what he finds, and it is common for large landowners to have extensive archaeological museums in their own homes. These landowners have contributed, in fact, most of the pre-Columbian artifacts found in our National Museum. But it is such a bad way to supply the museum. These sites should be excavated by qualified archaeologists. The ground would wait until we had the people and resources, but the landowners will not."

What is not legal is to try and sell the artifacts, or to transport them out of the country. Yet a source who had worked with the government (and who asked not to be identified) told me that the smuggling of artifacts was commonplace. "Many of the bulldozers in this country are owned by treasure hunters, and it is well-known to the government inner circle that some of the biggest exporters of artifacts are some of this country's most important ex-politicos. It is a big, big business. A great deal of money is involved."

It is a big business from which not only Costa Rica suffers, but all of Central and South America. The United States has entered into formal antiquities protection agreements with nations such as Peru and Mexico, and the adjoining countries are covered by the U.S. National Stolen Properties Law and the National Receiving Stolen Goods Law. Costa Rica has taken steps to protect itself with an artifact protection law authored by Quesada but, by his own admission, it has changed nothing. "If a person is caught leaving the country with even one small artifact, he can be taken immediately to jail and then sentenced to three or more years. But there are too many secluded regions in Costa Rica. Too many places for small planes to land and take off. And drug smugglers are the main concern of federal agents, not artifact smugglers."

I asked Quesada if he felt I was wrong to go to the site with my friend, and he echoes the rationalizations I would have employed anyway: "Your not going won't stop him. And perhaps it is something you should see."

In less than an hour, using only the machete, I uncovered four more jade figurines and a large stone jaguar's head, drilled through the center like a napkin holder. I do not like to think of the way I was that morning: a picture of greed, slicing at the earth with a long knife, sweating, thirsty, but absolutely focused on finding more. "Hah-day fever," I told Jesus as we finally hiked back down the hill toward the horses. I didn't add, "Dirty business," but I should have.

Jesus said, "Much work, but very exciting. Perhaps you can tell Bayardo how it is and he will come with me tomorrow."

That was a surprising thing to hear. Bayardo had never been to the hill?

"Not since the night the cook died," Jesus told me. "It was the cook who found this place and first discovered the hah-day."

Guatemala, *Guatemala*

The debate about the merits of packaged tours versus the freedom of autonomous travel has gotten ugly; the bickering and name calling have gone on long enough. Settling this matter requires the unbiased touch of one who does not entirely agree that all group tour clients are whining sheep spawn with the sensibilities of 50-year-old virgins, nor that all autonomous travelers are antisocial rogues with homicidal potential (Son of Sam, you may remember, assiduously avoided Caribbean cruises).

It is a difficult question with few easy answers, which is why, in the interest of harmony, I offer this paper, perhaps the only research effort on the subject. Employing several of the classic techniques of collation, I have used Guatemala as my *exempli gratia* because it is a foreign country ideally suited to both individual travel and group tours. To offer stark contrast between the two philosophies of travel, I went first to Guatemala as the member of a group tour. I ate when the group ate, slept when the group slept, and rode in my assigned seat on the bus. Once back in the United States, I then planned a second trip to Guatemala—but on my own. When I returned to that country, I followed my own instincts rather than a schedule and I profited and suffered accordingly.

Which trip was better? The results, I think, are unbiased and fair-spirited—even the sheep spawn who prefer packaged tours will agree. But, from this day-by-day comparison of journal entries, it is for you to judge whether or not the results are conclusive.

DAY ONE (GROUP TOUR)   Nine of us plus our guide meet for the first time at Miami International: eight free-lance writers and Carl, a former zoo curator. When it comes time to draw roommates, I'm the lucky one—I get Carl. Legitimate journalists are not supposed to accept the kind of tourism promotion this junket clearly is, and billeting with a zookeeper adds just the right sardonic touch. Everything is complimentary, from plane fare to food. Always quick with a rationalization, I tell Carl, "For me, this trip is strictly research." Carl, who seems so serious that I correctly guess he is also a bird-watcher, answers, "I couldn't afford anything but a group freebie either." On our flight to Guatemala City, our tour leader distributes literature. Most of us spend the time reading. One member offers to teach me needlepoint.

DAY ONE (SOLO TOUR)   If I am bound for Guatemala, what am I doing in Belize City? The answer is complicated, having to do with missed planes and planning errors no tour guide could possibly make and hope to survive. But let's check our maps: Belize adjoins Guatemala, and this nasty little port town offers rental cars. I had my eye on a nice Land Cruiser—one of those hulking four cylinders ideal for serious off-road head banging—but instead fell in with four British soldiers and two Gurkhas. Which is how I ended up here on Cay Caulker, a funky little coco palm island with a chickee restaurant that serves great lobster. I have met five American guys who also planned

Guatemala, Guatemala

to go to Guatemala. Apparently, it is not uncommon to set out for one Central American country only to miss and hit Belize.

○ ○ ○

DAY TWO (GROUP TOUR) Guatemala City; there is a summer-camp atmosphere as our tour group meets for breakfast and receives a briefing on this day's itinerary. An imposing list it is: a cathedral, a museum, an art gallery, a convent, and a textile factory; we are to visit them all before we leave for Lake Atitlán tomorrow. The only free time allowed was an hour after breakfast, so I decided to spend part of it jogging. Ten minutes from the hotel, though, an old malady struck—brain transmigration—and, upon revisiting reality, I found myself hopelessly lost in what is known as Old City, near the Mercado Central where the mountain people bring their vegetables and beans and coffee to sell. By the time I made it back to the hotel, I had missed the bus and most of the day's itinerary. Surprisingly, several group members told me later that they would like to join me on tomorrow's run.

○ ○ ○

DAY TWO (SOLO TOUR) I have nothing against mercenaries from Nepal, but these Gurkhas make me uneasy with their gleeful tales of beheading Argentine soldiers. Yet they do not trouble me as much as Humpridge, one of the Americans. Humpridge, his friends tell me, likes to cap a night of beery excess by running away, daring his buddies to find him. These hide-and-seek games, they tell me, have crossed the borders of countries; involved local police, outraged fathers, and nursing cattle; and sometimes take days.

Why do they bother chasing him, I want to know.

Because, they tell me, Humpridge adds spice to the game by taking their passports and money with him.

Humpridge, a former football captain at an Ivy League university, listens to these tales cheerfully, then sums up: "I like Third World countries. They're *fun.*"

The five Americans want to know if I want to join them on their trip to Guatemala. Have they confused me with a crazy person? I ask them.

Of course I'll go. Who wouldn't?

○ ○ ○

DAY THREE (GROUP TOUR)   Our group has its own bus; a white and green air-conditioned number with a microphone so we can hear the guide. I like our guide. He knows all kinds of things and keeps me busy taking notes. Also, he deals swiftly with the military roadblocks that are common in this country. A few bills and fewer words, and we are passed right through. On this bus, the men sit in the back and the women ride in the front. Is this bus an Oldsmobile? I ask Carl. Are we imitating Miami retirees for a reason? Carl says the arrangement has more to do with my habit of spitting sunflower seeds out the window.

We have arrived at Lake Atitlán, a great green pool beneath volcanic peaks. We are visiting the lake to learn about a rare, endangered bird, the giant pied-billed grebe, known locally as the poc. This small flightless creature faces almost certain extinction for reasons our guide will tell us once we are on the ferry. We are a somber group of bird lovers as we depart the bus.

○ ○ ○

DAY FOUR (SOLO TOUR)   Thanks to these five Americans, I may have discovered the perfect way to travel. Yesterday we rented a pickup truck in Belize City, then we each contributed $50 to a group fund. From that fund, we purchased coolers, ice, food, and bottled beverages. When the money is gone, we will each contribute more money. Result: no bookkeeping, plus the back of this truck is loaded with comfortable seats (the coolers) plus many interesting things to drink.

Guatemala, Guatemala

Riding in the back of a truck through the Maya Mountains (which extend from Belize into Guatemala) is a wonderful thing. The smells of river sloughs, of village cooking fires, of mountain cloud forests hit one full in the face, and children, standing beside their mothers washing clothes in fast rivers, grin at us and shout in Mayan. The only bad thing is that village militia spot us easily, and we are often detained at roadblocks by stern government troops who frisk us and paw through our bags. Only Humpridge seems to enjoy this, for he jokes with the soldiers (though they don't understand his English) and he holds his passport playfully over their heads, making them leap for it. "See?" says Humpridge. "They won't shoot."

DAY FOUR (GROUP TOUR) One of a number of reasons the small, flightless poc will soon be extinct, our guide tells us, is that many years ago some Pan Am pilots imported largemouth bass into the lake, and now those fish, grown gigantic, are eating the baby birds. The idea of swaggering aviators despoiling this place with exotic fish outrages my fellow bird-watchers. Well, my heart isn't made of Formica, and I feel bad for the bird, but I am also very happy that someone had the good sense to bring a spinning reel and a pack rod (me). While the tour group bemoans these evil fish, I can actually do something about them—if I can just find a way to sneak away. Trouble is, we are on the buddy system here, and Carl is my buddy. But just before lunch, Carl provides me my opportunity, saying he wants to hike into the mountains to do some bird-watching. Great, I tell him. Take your time. Then I hustle straight to the little nearby Mayan village to see if I can rent a boat—and there is Carl holding a fishing rod. He smiles sheepishly and he says, "I don't know about you, but when they started talking about giant bass, my first inclination was to have a 200-horse skeeter eater shipped up here, a bushel of crank baits, and tell those poc people I will personally bust my butt to save the little bastard."

Carl, like me, is a conservationist.

Batfishing in the Rainforest

○ ○ ○

DAY FIVE (SOLO TOUR)   Our trip was stalled at dusk when more than a dozen armed men—government militia—stepped out of the bushes, stopped our truck, and searched us. Coincidentally, our last spare tire went flat at the same time. Not so coincidentally, we ran out of bottled beverages about an hour later. These soldiers are not bad guys, and they apologized for the thoroughness of their earlier search. Clearly, though, we are in a tough spot here: We are out of beer. Also, we need to find a tire. But first things first. One of the soldiers confided to us that he knew the local guerilla leader who, he was certain, would sell us some beer. I am not an expert in politics, but visiting a guerilla leader in the dead of night with a government soldier as a guide did not seem a good plan. Humpridge, though, was charmed by the idea and we immediately set off on foot. There was no moon, but there were stars through the trees, and we followed the dirt road for more than a mile until we came to a thatched-roof hut that also served as a local *tienda*. The soldier pounded on the door until the guerilla leader answered, carrying a lighted candle. Humpridge said to the soldier, "Tell this guy that if he doesn't sell us some beer we'll kill his cow." Humpridge was pointing to a donkey tied beneath a tree, but it didn't matter because neither the soldier nor the storekeeper understood him. The man sold us 40 bottles of beer, which he separated into two burlap bags. I took one bag, Humpridge the other—and then somehow, on the walk back, he disappeared. Just fell behind and disappeared. I was amazed. How could a 6′ 2″, 240-pound former linebacker carrying a bag of clanking bottles just vanish? The other Americans tell me they are surprised he waited this long.

I hope Humpridge returns soon, because tomorrow we plan to head for the Maya ruins at Tikal, and we'll almost certainly need our passports and some money to buy tires.

○ ○ ○

The two journals go on. We caught no bass. During a lapse in judgment, though, Carl did buy two live chickens at a Mayan village across the lake, and our guide told more than one group member that I was an evil influence. We found Humpridge (minus the beer) and we made it to Tikal. Both trips ended well, though I think these notes clearly show that it doesn't much matter how you hit the open road—just as long as you occasionally hit it.

The Strange Mammals
of Ningaloo

*a*ustralia is better known for its oddities than its subtleties, though the language can assume qualities of both. On Coral Bay in western Australia, Davy, Earl, and Harry know I'm a jurno but give me an invite down to their campo for sammies and a barbie anyway.

The barbie is at their campo: a stilthouse built among sand dunes overlooking Coral Bay, which is 600 empty miles north of Perth and 700 emptier miles southwest of Broome in a region called Gascoyne. Much of the land that lies between is desert and barren coast, an area best known for the wild bottle-nosed dolphins that come to swim with humans at Monkey Mia, and for its 160 miles of living coral bank, though these things are hardly known at all outside Australia. Like everyone who visits the country, I have come for the land and for its people, but my main interest is this coral reef. I first heard of it while in Perth for the America's Cup races: unexpected stories of a largely unexplored sea region; one of those wild places to which one must hurry before it has been diminished by a shrinking world.

The coral formations, I was told, rivaled those of the Great Barrier Reef and, because few spearfishermen had visited it, big fish were commonly seen—a rare thing, for even remote reefs have suffered from spearfishermen or from commercial collectors of tropical fish, who, in much of Asia and parts of the South Pacific, use sodium cyanide to stun aquarium species. Much of the reef (the Ningaloo, it is called) was still virgin, I was assured, not only because the reef is isolated, but because the reef itself is a biological oddity. Nearly all of the world's major coral banks are found on the eastern coasts of large land masses, not the western. Perhaps because of this, the size and importance of the massive Ningaloo reef were, until only recently, underestimated and unappreciated.

But such a reef could not go unappreciated—and unexplored—for long. The Western Australia Tourism Commission, anxious to capitalize on international attention invited by the Cup races, was now including information on Ningaloo in its brochures. And only a few months before my return to Australia, the Gascoyne's first dive shop was opened—a one-man beach rental in the settlement of Coral Bay, population 25. Which is why I have come to Coral Bay and why, now, I am accompanying Davy, Earl, and Harry to their campo for a barbie, carrying their esky, which, they insist, is a duty entrusted to few outsiders and illustrates their faith in me. I'm flattered, naturally, and wrestle the cooler up the wooden steps alone—the damn thing must weigh a hundred pounds.

Their stilthouse is a man's place with wooden bunks and a hole in one wall the size of a fist. Beyond the beer cans stacked on the windowsill I can see the demarcation of Ningaloo Reef where 30-foot waves slide through the light of a new moon, then implode in a haze of their own green luminescence. A gale has blown up and, because of the big seas, I have not been able to get outside the reef to dive. Instead, I have spent my days exploring the aboriginal sites, enjoying the best in-shore snorkeling of my life, and accepting dinner invitations from various western Australians, a people who are as startlingly informal as they are friendly.

"Light the barbie and put those nasty snaggers on," says a voice. "I could eat the bum off a duck if it flew by low."

Davy, Earl, and Harry are businessmen from Perth. Judging from their clothes and their new four-wheel-drive vehicles, they are financially comfortable, yet they have ignored the more popular and populated coastal resorts for what is, perhaps, one of the least traveled shorelines of the modern world. That's what they like about it, they tell me: The Gascoyne, particularly Coral Bay, doesn't have blinkin' tourists all over the blinkin' beaches, nor a bunch of ankle-biters or surfies with their norks hanging out. The fishing, the diving, the seclusion, they say, make it a good place to go when a man is rooted.

"You understand that?" asks Davy.

No. But what I *am* beginning to understand is why, in 1982, the Miami Film Festival committee decided all Australian films should use English subtitles.

Davy says, "Another thing: In Sydney, it's Australia, but here it's not. I mean, you don't say Australia."

Oh?

"No, You say 'Oz.' I'm a bloke from West Oz. You're in West Oz. At a barbie. Before a piss-up. Because the bloody wind is on the bung and we can't get out in the bloody boats."

"But with a lovely stock of tinnies," adds Harry. He has the esky open again, rummaging among the shaved ice and cans of beer with an expression of pure affection.

"Which are to be pounded?" I hazard.

"Good onya," says Davy.

"He's catching on!"

Harry hands me another Emu. "Welcome to Oz," he says.

○ ○ ○

Between Perth and the port town of Geraldton, a drive of about 200 miles, the famous Australian outback that one expects does not exist.

It is rural country, sometimes desolate, but the hills roll green with fenced pasture, and there are farmhouses in the valleys and vineyards with wineries of old stone.

Beyond Geraldton, though, the land changes. Green becomes brown, then burnt orange: a harsh ferrous color as if paint has saturated the soil and dried to dust. This is big country; a landscape of horizons marked only by cloud shadows and their accelerating contrails of sunlight.

Also, the road changes in name from the Brand Highway to the Great Northwest Coastal Highway and, as if sobered by the nomenclature, straightens into a no-nonsense conduit built for speed, not sightseeing. Traffic is sparse and driving, already uninteresting, becomes monotonous. I traveled with two friends: John from Alabama and Charlie from uptown Manhattan—a potentially volatile combination that had long since been defused by previous trips and a sensible division of responsibility. Charlie always drives because, having survived years of Manhattan traffic, his passengers concede he can probably survive anywhere. John always navigates because, having dealt with many New Yorkers lost en route to Florida, he is more keenly aware that people who can miss whole oceans are also apt to miss turns.

On the Northwest Coastal Highway, though, there are no turns and very few curves. So we passed the hours listening to Australian Broadcasting Company radio and commenting on the two things there are to see: wildflowers and road kill. The road kill of western Australia can be divided into two categories: things that look like dead kangaroos and probably are, and things that don't look like dead kangaroos but probably are. Noting road kill may seem like a grim way to wile away the hours but, in truth, warm asphalt on a cool night can provide travelers with a better sampling of fauna than the local zoo, and certainly better than the few live sightings one can expect to make while driving through the daylight heat of a dry land. We had seen three emus— gawky ratite birds, like ostriches—feeding in the shade, but no live kangaroos in two days of driving. Yet it was unusual to drive five miles without seeing a dead one: big animals shrunken and mummified by the sun. Sometimes we would stop and inspect the remains. While I tried to decide whether it was a red or grey kangaroo, or a wallaby, John would stand there waving at the flies and say something like, "Hoo-whee, this place got enough bugs for three countries and two boats," or, "After seein' this place, I figure these kangaroos didn't get killed, they committed suicide. Took the Toyota cure for boredom."

No one can drive the shield-and-mountain desert of west-central Australia without being impressed by its harshness. Flies swarm in the shade of wind-tattered salt bush and even fimetic beetles hide from the heat beneath scabs of sheep dung. It seems an impossible place for humans to survive, but they do survive, living and working at lonesome outposts such as Billabong Roadhouse and Overlander: truck-stop-type places with lunch counters and fuel and signs that read: *Please Don't Ask for Fresh Water. We Have None to Spare.* All vehicles in this region are equipped with big steel bumpers called 'roo guards, and once, around the pool table at Billabong, I heard men joking about how many kangaroos they had hit the night before—the tone of their laughter implying the contempt they felt for any creature that could multiply so easily in a land that is so hard. Only vermin could procreate at such a pace, or so their attitudes seemed to suggest—one of Australia's many dichotomies, for the animal held so dear as a national symbol is treated by some as road sport and viewed with scorn.

All of these elements, when fused by a long day on the road, might create a mood of gloominess not even beer could dent but for one thing: wildflowers. In spring (September through November) the wildflowers of western Australia are spectacular. You travel miles of scrub and hot, flat highway only to top a rise where, unexpectedly, the desert disappears beneath a fresh patina of blue or white or lavender petals. The dominant color varies but always pales toward the horizon, its continuity broken only by pockets of competing species—flowers of bright red or yellow, like patches of sunlight. Even if you are not an admirer of flowers, it's a refreshing thing to come upon. There are

Orange Morrisons, Black Kangaroos Paws, Cockies Tongues, Fringe Lillies, and others probably not in the book from which I am getting these names. The names don't matter. To pass through a region where flowers blend with the far curvature of earth is worth the getting there, and all the more striking because it makes no sense that things so bright and delicate would grow here.

There are gentler lands.

O   O   O

In 1964, according to a Tourism Commission press release, a woman waded into the water off the Peron Peninsula, offered an approaching bottle-nosed dolphin a fish to eat, and the dolphin accepted it from her hand. The dolphin, which locals named Charlie, returned each day to feed, and other dolphins soon followed. These dolphins came not just to eat but because they were as curious as the people who came to pet them, and so began, says the release, a unique interaction between sea mammals and humans that continues to this day.

This is a good story, but the story told by some residents of Denham (the peninsula's main town) is better because it makes more sense, and it's probably even true. Hang around the Shark Bay Hotel bar, and patrons may explain to you that, back in the early 1960s, the only reason someone not off their nong would live in Monkey Mia was to make a living fishing. Fishing was top lurk, shit-hot; very good. During the big runs, commercial netters were busier than brickies in Beirut, that's how good it was, and netters took to heaving out less desirable fish while motoring homeward. Bottle-nosed dolphins, attracted by the windfall, began to follow along, and one dolphin— Charlie—would follow the boats clear back to the dock. As Charlie grew used to the routine, fishermen began to feed him by hand, and then so did the wives and children of the fishermen. In time, other dolphins began to accompany the animal called Charlie, just as human outsiders began to join the residents of the Peron Peninsula, swimming among and feeding the dolphins.

The Strange Mammals of Ningaloo

According to several U.S. marine biologists with whom I spoke, it is unusual for a lone wild dolphin to solicit fish from humans on a regular basis, but it is not unique. There have been similar cases documented off the coasts of England, New Zealand, Africa, and the Caribbean. But for an entire pod of dolphins to return daily to the same tiny stretch of beach, and then endure petting in exchange for a few fish, *is* unique. Monkey Mia is the only place in the world where such interaction is known to occur and, as a result, residents of the Peron Peninsula are no longer considered to be off their nongs. In 1985, the 60 miles of dirt road to Denham were surfaced, a hardtop road to Monkey Mia is being built, and a thriving tourist trade is now anticipated. But don't expect a plush resort waiting. Monkey Mia consists of a small camper park, a ranger station, and a dock. Denham is one of those transitory fishing villages with gale-frayed palms and houses built out-of-square, as if no one expected to stay very long. There's a take-out restaurant that advertises *Cheap Food* on a wooden sign, and a place with video games for teenagers.

My friend and I stayed at the Shark Bay Hotel, a motel-type facility with plywood rooms and air conditioners that rattled on their window mounts. The best thing about the place was that it had the only bar in town and everyone congregated there. The next morning, Monkey Mia, a 15-mile drive, seemed pristine in comparison; a place of sand dunes and open sea.

Monkey Mia (pronounced "Monkey Mire" by Aussies) was a side trip for me; a stop I didn't particularly want to make on the long drive to Ningaloo Reef. The wind was already beginning to gust randomly from the northwest, then the southeast, and few things make a boater or diver more nervous than a nervous wind. Besides, from what one reads about Monkey Mia, one gets the impression it's a cross between Sea World and a petting zoo; an attraction certain to disappoint. It does not. You pay your $5 car fee, walk to the beach, and there they are: bottle-nosed dolphins cruising the shallows, spouting, turning on their sides to break the barrier of water with their large eyes, staring at you as surely as you have come to stare at them. It was at Monkey Mia that I got the surest sense of why western Australia is, at once, promoting and protecting the Gascoyne region, this peculiar Oz.

There were five dolphins off the beach the morning we arrived and about a dozen people, most of whom had walked over from the camper park. A volunteer ranger in Wellington boots kept a watchful eye, for there was to be no feeding on this morning. Head ranger Sharon Gosper told me they had cut back on feedings because they didn't want the dolphins to become dependent on people, and also because their researchers felt the males were burning excess energy by continually herding new females into the area. "It tended to make the males very tense and edgy because the new females would try to escape. The males would chase them back in a very aggressive way, and that deterred the regular females from coming in."

The grand old man of Monkey Mia dolphins is Wilf Mason. Wilf and his wife Hazel built the camper park in the mid-1970s and, working with other concerned Australians, founded the Dolphin Welfare Foundation, which is largely responsible for the funding and the organization that now monitors and protects the animals. You can find Wilf most any day doing odd jobs around his "caravan park," but he's always willing to talk about the creatures he obviously cares so much about—and that also keep his park booked months in advance.

Unlike some biologists, Wilf doesn't believe the dolphins come to Monkey Mia just for an easy feed. "Too bloody often, I've seen a dolphin carry in a fish and give it to some stranger standing in the water gawking at it. Like a gift. There're plenty of fish in this area, and they don't need us to feed them. I think this section of beach must have been their area years back, and they're naturally just as curious as we are. They like to interact with people; play fetch with a piece of seaweed, or come up behind someone in the water and scare the daylights out of them. I've seen 'em do it, just plain full of piss and Gunga Din.

"Over the years, a real trust has been built up, and that's all the more reason we need to protect them from the very, very few oddballs who'd want to hurt them. Before the rangers, some of the usual sadistic bullshit went on: beer or cigarettes down their blowholes. But no more. We Aussies know how to take care of our own."

The importance of protection became clear to me when I went to the beach and waded with the dolphins. As a Sanibel, Florida, fishing guide, I see a similar species of dolphin nearly every day from my boat. But to walk among these big animals, to have one bring you a bit of shell or to roll on its side so that it might inspect you, is an entirely different experience and hits at an unexpected level. But I was not nearly so affected as a man in the water near me. He was an older man in his sixties and, because emotion registered so clearly in his voice, I listened as he told the ranger that he was from New Zealand and had saved for many years to make this trip—just to see the dolphins. His name was Timmons MacDonald, and he explained to me later that he had been a fisherman in New Zealand where his small community also had a dolphin they could feed by hand; a dolphin they called Pelorus Jack.

"After every fishing trip, heading home, that dolphin would lead us right back in through the reefs. It was like a job to him. Fog, rain it didn't matter. I don't know how he knew we were coming, but he knew. The town built a monument to him, that's how much we came to depend on Jack." MacDonald stopped to scratch the belly of a dolphin: a small man in a suit coat, up to his knees in water and smiling as he said, "Beauties, aren't they? Clicking at us—that's how they talk, you know. Just like our Jack used to talk before some bloody, bloody fool shot him."

○ ○ ○

The day we arrived at Coral Bay, the wind swung as if on a pendulum, southeast, northwest, southeast and finally held from the northwest, gaining momentum, it seemed, from the new stability and gusting to 40 knots. A half mile from shore, waves rolled toward the motel, the camper park, and the few houses that make up the community in slow green rows, lucent and big as ships, only to collapse beneath their own weight at the line of reef. Coral Bay, protected by the reef, was calm, but the few boats at anchor leaned on their lines, shifting like weather vanes, and men on the beach said things like, "It's a week for cracking tinnies, not fishing."

The reef runs, roughly, from Exmouth to Carnarvon, but the weather would be the same all up an down the coast, and we decided to wait it out where we were. Coral Bay suited our preference for isolated places, plus it is small and neat with a superb network of bush trails that crisscross remote sand dunes and bluffs at the edge of the sea—great for jogging.

That's what I did at Coral Bay: I jogged. Each morning I ran south down the beach and beyond the bluffs, carrying my diving mask. In the afternoons, I ran north to Skeleton Bay and back. When a patch of shallow reef caught my interest, I swam out. The only escape from the wind was here, underwater: a world as powerful in color and life as the Gascoyne is powerful in its sustained and energized desolation. A meter beneath the surface, there were staghorn forests, delicate branching corals, purple sea fans, and golden brain corals the size of vaults. Schools of big snappers and speckled butterfly fish hung motionless in the reef surge like huge drifting mobiles, and there seemed no end, no single break, in the maze of coral and color and life. It was maddening to think that beyond the breakers, only a few hundred yards away, were the reef's deeper, unseen places and probably some of the best scuba diving in the world.

"The wind is gonna blow for at least another week; could be a cyclone's coming," Clives Wilkins, manager of the hotel, told me. We had already stayed two days longer than we'd planned and, in a gesture of either pity or kindness, Wilkins had helped me break up the days, giving me history tours of the area. He had even driven me to a prehistoric aboriginal site, a small sand pocket beneath the cliffs littered with broken shell implements and the scorched bones of turtles and fish. It was a place, he said, he had shown no one but his wife.

The Strange Mammals of Ningaloo

Once we took a small boat across the coral banks to the inside edge of the reef. From shore, the waves had looked big, but here I saw oceanic waves as I have never seen them: a great, sliding mountain range of water, 30-feet high and white crested; an endless emerald city that mapped in sea foam the coral heads and troughs I had come 15,000 miles to see.

"You're just gonna have to be satisfied with snorkeling," Wilkins told me.

He was right.

The Sickness of Peru

t was 7:01 p.m. when the first bomb exploded, knocking out the power in the Peruvian mountain town of Huancayo. I know the exact time because I have one of those watches that light up when you press a button. There was a thundering noise, windows rattled, the power went out, and I pressed the button on my watch because when you are sitting on the stool in the bathroom of a chintzy hotel, even a tiny light seems like a friendly thing.

A transformer had blown up, that's what I hoped. But then there was the firecracker pop of automatic weapons and muffled screams from somewhere outside. Then three more explosions in quick succession. Faulty wiring and power surges do not cause such noises—this even I knew, sitting in the dark, suffering the effects of altitude sickness and Peruvian microbes.

I fumbled around until I found my flashlight and clothes, then stepped out into the hall. I was on the second floor of a three-story hotel. Two men sat in comfortable chairs looking through a broad window, watching Huancayo's municipal plaza—Siskel and Ebert reviewing the panic below. In the red and blue flare of police lights, people were running: strobe light caricatures frozen every few yards in mid-stride. Minutes before there had been several hundred people in the plaza listening to the music of mountain flutes, celebrating Huancayo's 416th anniversary. Now the plaza was nearly empty; the sound of gunfire close and continuous. There was another explosion, and one of the men looked up, letting his eyes settle on my flashlight; a covetous look. He said, *"bombas,"* and the other man said, *"terroristas,"* to which I felt like replying, "No shit, Sherlock?" for I was in a mood. In the space of 48 hours I had traveled from sea level to nearly 16,000 feet. I'd had goat's-head soup for breakfast, and some college-type kid had spit on my shoes. I'd paid a girl I shouldn't have trusted to take me fishing and we'd ended up two hours from town at a restaurant that served trout. Then, on the streets of Huancayo, two udder-dogs dressed as men had walked up and tried to stab me—not a word of warning, just walked up and stabbed me. Now there was a running gun battle going on outside in the plaza and soon, I felt sure, Siskel and Ebert would be asking to borrow my flashlight. Fat chance.

"Sendero," said one of the men, meaning the terrorists, the Shining Path. They are a plague, he said: him lounging there in his chair trying to ingratiate himself, telling me he had work to do in his room if he only had a light, while I crouched low, fearful of stray bullets and expecting a bomb to go off inside the hotel at any moment. "They are the sickness of Peru," he told me.

The sickness of Peru is a multifaceted thing and I, for one, was suffering the garden variety. I headed downstairs, the beam of my flashlight glazing the banister with feverish coronas and casting huge shadows. In the lobby, the clerk had lighted oil lamps; guests carried candles. A policeman and three other men stood inside the hotel's bolted double doors as if they might soon have to brace their shoulders against it. The policeman held an Uzi submachine gun; the others had revolvers and blackjacks. The windows were shuttered and I followed the milling guests toward the dining room: a Maglite among candles at some bizarre Mass or funeral procession; yet the atmosphere was more like that of a slumber party. These were mostly professional people from Lima, businessmen and doctors on holiday, and they behaved as if the explosions were thunder, the popping sounds rain on the roof. I, the only American, sat alone at a table, hating them because I was scared. I was shaking. How could they laugh? How could they eat? But then a bomb went off so close that a window in the dining room shattered, plaster fell, and several women screamed. For an instant, just an instant, the sickness of Peru was in them, too. I could see it in the way the men jumped to their feet as if to challenge the noise to a fistfight— a reaction of pure anxiety that quickly faded to embarrassment. The headwaiter nodded at the busboy, motioning with his head, and the busboy went to the piano and began to play so badly that it took me a moment to recognize the tune. As the kid played, the room slowly gathered its veneer of gaiety while gunfire still echoed outside. Men reached for wineglasses; women leaned to light their cigarettes. I sat there listening, studying the plaster that had fallen into my asparagus soup, studying the knuckle I had split on the guys who had attacked me earlier that day, feeling feverish and lost in a room of bad theater, thinking: *Christ, they should pitch a tent over this whole damn country and charge admission.*

The guys upstairs didn't need a flashlight. The kid at the piano was playing "As Time Goes By," and there wasn't a building in Peru big enough to hold all the usual suspects. What Siskel and Ebert needed was popcorn.

$$\bigcirc \quad \bigcirc \quad \bigcirc$$

Here's what literature from the Peruvian Tourist Board says about the highest standard-gauge train trip in the world:

> The central railway is regarded as one of the wonders of South America. It will take you through 66 tunnels, 59 bridges, zig-zagging up the steep mountainsides whenever a straight ascent is impossible. The trip from Lima to Huancayo (332 kilometers) makes several interesting stops in interesting villages, and passes through one of the

highest inhabited points in the world, Alianza and Venturosa mines (4,775 meters). The scenery through the Andes is ruggedly magnificent. The trip takes about 10 hours. Lunch is served in the carriage.

Well, this sounds like fun: bridges, scenery, lunch, and maybe some llamas too, up there on the ruggedly magnificent mountainsides. But the tourist literature glosses over many of the side attractions and misses the flavor of the train ride entirely. Colorful stuff like projectile vomiting in the aisles and children sobbing hysterically at the dizzying switchbacks. Also, toilets that aren't up to the work load and loose chickens banging around the carriages, gone berserk from altitude depression and maybe the knowledge that lunch can't start until the cook gets them stopped. Nor does the literature say that beer isn't sold. In hindsight, the reason is obvious: the concessionaires just fear that, somewhere between San Mateo (3,215 meters) and Casapalca (4,153 meters), a drunken contingent of passengers might grab the engineer by the throat and force him to turn his hell-train around and point it back toward earth.

All in all, the ride between Lima and Huancayo seemed a Third World dream trip; a safe platform from which to peer into the maw of this lunatic country without being swallowed by it. Best of all, it strayed nowhere near Cusco or the Inca ruins at Machu Picchu, places where grass no longer grows because of all the tourist tromping or maybe the wilting brain waves of Shirley MacLaine and other reincarnation victims. The train trip would be to us armchair adventurers what the Concorde might be to the Club Med crowd. Just a scent of hot breath and maybe a few stains. I signed up without being asked twice.

But there were complications. A disinformation artist from the Peruvian Tourist Board called and said my trip had to be postponed because summer rains had washed out one of the bridges. Well, one must be flexible. Then he called just before my second try and said the rains had done it again; another bridge gone. I didn't realize at the time I was playing Gomer Pyle to his Vince Carter, saying *Goll-e-e-e-e* to bald-faced lies contrived to drive a wedge between me and what was really going on. It wasn't until the Peruvian winter that I finally arrived in Lima, and one of the first things I asked was how were things in the mountains after all those terrible flash floods. I got blank stares in return. Rainfall had been heavy, but it hadn't damaged the bridges.

Then what did?

Now I got shrugs, which, one soon learns, is the accepted way of avoiding unpleasant topics in Peru. In this instance, the unpleasant topic was *Sendero*.

Shazam.

○ ○ ○

In Lima, in winter, it never rains, but the sun does not shine. A perpetual gloom hangs over the city; a yellow mist known locally as *garúa* that dilutes the sky and makes visual approaches to Jorge Chavez International nigh near impossible. On an AeroPeru jet, we dropped through the fog and banged the landing strip without a glimpse of the city—a disconcerting thing, since I had been steering with my toes since the storm over Panama and thought, for one horrible tight-sphincter moment, I'd collided with the Andes.

Tight-sphincter moments are not uncommon in Lima. Since conquistador Francisco Pizarro founded the city in 1535, *Limenos* have endured so many earthquakes, revolutions, bombings, and financial collapses that, after more than 20 generations of living on the edge, evolution should have long since coded them with a distinctive way of walking. I arrived in Lima early in the evening on a weekday and, on the way to Hotel Limatambo in the suburb of Miraflores, found the streets strewn with rocks and the walls splattered with fresh graffiti. "There has been a celebration here," Roxana Suarez, a tourist board representative, told me, straight-faced, as the driver of our ragged VW bug dodged the litter. The celebration had, in fact, been a demonstration by students from the University of San Marcos, the oldest university in the Western Hemisphere and a traditional stronghold of Communist students and professors. The students had burned buses and stoned police before retreating to the campus, which, as the grounds of an autonomous university, are beyond the normal legal reach of Peruvian authorities.

"A celebration?" I asked Suarez. The street graffiti read: *Long Live the Armed Struggle; Long Live Sendero; Death to the Oppressor Swine*—rhetoric not generally associated with fraternity bashes and party animals.

"Yes," said Suarez, "Lima is a very happy place."

Before dropping me at my hotel, Suarez abandoned her posturing long enough to warn me not to put my duffel bag down "even for a moment" or to leave my hotel until she arrived the next day to take me to the train station. But, within an hour of checking in, I was back on the streets smelling of cheap shampoo, a *Cristal* beer in hand, anxious to get the feel of this happy city.

Nearly one third of Peru's population—six million people—lives in Lima. The striations of class and wealth begin with the great guarded town houses at the edge of the sea, then move inland toward downtown Lima in abrupt gradations of middle class, lower middle class, then to the massive rind of slums on the eastern edge of the city. Nearly two million Limenos live in these shanty towns called *pueblos jóvenes,* or young towns, because the houses, made of cardboard and pilfered lumber, are thrown up as quickly as the elements and overpopulation destroy them. I headed for the center of the city, first on foot, then by cab, through the suburbs with their barred windows and barking guard dogs, then skirted the slums close enough to see the bright cooking fires. The *Rio Rimac,* the historic water source for this city built on coastal desert, was a glittering black strand that smelled of petroleum and cabbage.

Walking the streets of downtown Lima, one gets the sense that whatever is wrong with Peru nests here—a naive notion that this country's many problems can be distilled into a single sensory unit, yet the feeling is tangible; a dark immanence that clings to the narrow streets and the ornate, crumbling architecture. I walked along the mall that joins the Plaza San Martin with the Plaza de Armas, past vendors selling fruits and flowers from bicycles, past Indio women begging beneath bright store windows dotted with posters advertising Jordache jeans. Just before reaching the Palace of Justice, though, I was pointedly turned back by one of the many heavily armed policemen who patrol the streets. He refused explanation, but I later learned that it was due to bomb threats. In July of 1987, a car packed with dynamite exploded while being hauled away from the nearby Sheraton Hotel and, in the same month, a Toyota loaded with dynamite and chemical explosives was discovered just outside the airport's international departure area. Such threats are not taken lightly, and the park, which had been laid out by the Spanish in 1535, was now closed to pedestrian traffic.

I turned north, noting the graffiti as I walked: Every wall and fence in Lima, it seems, is covered with slogans in candy-colored spray paint. Revolution is promised; Sendero or M.R.T.A. is the savior of the people (M.R.T.A. stands for Tupac Amaru Revolutionary Movement, a left-wing organization younger than Sendero and, thus far, less violent). All must ready themselves for struggle; all must prepare. Policemen backdropped by the graffiti, swaggering with their Uzis, seemed ready; the sparse sidewalk traffic—men and women hurrying with their packages as if anxious to be off the streets—less so.

In a country as poor as Peru, the desperate posturing of tourist board representatives is understandable, but Lima is anything but the happy place described by Roxana Suarez. In countenance, it is a city under siege in a nation that is at war; not a war that rages, but one that crackles along at unexpected times and in unexpected places. *Sendero Luminoso,* the Shining Path, is committed to bringing Peru to its knees—politically and economically—because, in the words of *El Diario* (the newspaper most closely associated with Sendero), "the people's cultural revolution can only succeed if built upon the graves of the oppressors."

These are not fun-loving folks, and Sendero's tactics are utterly ruthless—more ruthless and lawless, even, than those of the Peruvian military.

O   O   O

The Sendero movement began at the National University of San Cristobal in the Peruvian mountain department (state) of Ayacucho, about 200 miles southeast of Lima. The university was founded to educate the children of mountain Indians, with an emphasis on studies that would help them contribute to the Andean region—teaching, nursing, and agriculture. Quechua, the principal Indian language, was a required course. By the mid-1960s, though, the university's staff, all political leftists, were teaching revolution, led by pro-Mao Communist Abimael Guzman, a philosophy professor. Peru's Indians have historically been treated as animal-class citizens, and were receptive to any ideology that promised change. A generation of Cristobal graduates was sent back to mountain towns to teach grade-school students the gospel of Mao and violent overthrow. Then, in 1978, Guzman and his followers went underground to begin the fight.

Sendero's first attack was on a voting station: They burned it to demonstrate their hatred for democracy. A few months later, Limenos awoke to find dead dogs hanging from the city's lampposts—the "dogs of capitalism," according to the accompanying graffiti. But this was timid stuff compared to the violence soon embraced by the party line: the public executions of village officials and their families; the calculated murder of men, women, and even schoolchildren accused of not being sympathetic to the Sendero cause. In one mountain village attacked by Sendero, 60 townspeople were killed. Authorities discovered old men, women, and children huddled in the town church where they had been found by the Senderistas and hacked to death with axes.

In the ten years since Guzman went underground, the Shining Path has become one of the most feared yet secretive revolutionary movements in history. Sendero has allowed no interviews with journalists and makes no public claims for violent acts. Its soldiery is largely high school and college-age products of Guzman's educational seeding program begun 20 years before. They are said to adhere to a strict moral code—no drinking, no smoking—and they are as dedicated to secrecy as they are to violence. Nor is the military anxious to publicize Sendero's atrocities for, in the international community, they are often viewed as symptomatic of a failing government and, worse, might impact on tourist dollars depended upon by an impoverished people.

As a result, in the language of disinformation adopted by desperate public officials, the work of Sendero is sometimes credited to flash floods, heavy rains, lightning strikes, and similar acts of God.

O O O

The 7 a.m. train from Lima to Huancayo left 45 minutes late, which is right on time by Peruvian standards. Passengers had to pass through two checkpoints where police searched luggage—better security than at the Lima airport where I had twice set off metal detectors with my camera case but was ignored each time by two giggling policewomen.

I was traveling round-trip first class, a good investment at $5 U.S., because beyond the coupling in econo-class, arrangements looked lively: squashed elbows and faces mashed against the storm-door window, and strange grunting noises too, as if livestock might be involved. In comparison, first class was fairly comfortable: 44 people on 22 vinyl bench seats. We made a slow, jolting start as yellow fog swirled outside the windows and the train gained speed, passing through the bewildering poverty of Lima's eastern slums. An old woman holding her skirt up as she squatted behind a bush locked onto me with her rheumy eyes; naked children with distended stomachs peered up from trash piles and yanked at the air, demanding the engineer sound his horn. In contrast, the poverty of the countryside into which we were soon transported seemed pristine: women washing clothes on the rocks of the Rimac River as men lugged bundles of sticks up steep roads.

The literature says the train trip takes about 10 hours. My two trips averaged out at about 12 and, under such circumstances, sitting shoulder to shoulder like kids on a bus, there is little to do but read, look at the scenery, and visit with fellow riders. The scenery is rugged, just like the books say, but to describe it as magnificent is overly generous. There are no snow-capped peaks, just bald mountains streaked with mineral deposits and sluice scars. Yellow flowers called *retana* grow along the tracks, and the small rivers that edge the isolated villages flow bright orange with mineral runoff, for many of the villages have grown up around the massive mining projects the railroad serves.

But the trip is not without drama—largely due to a physiological phenomenon known as altitude sickness, a condition caused by lack of oxygen in the blood and tissues due to low atmospheric pressure. Quick ascents without proper acclimatization can result in faintness, nausea, loss of night vision, bizarre mood swings, and even death due to cerebral edema. I had done my reading, though, and knew that the medical prophylactic was to go easy on liquids and take actazolamide tablets, which are sold as Diamox. Unfortunately, I'd lost my Diamox somewhere between Miami and the beer cooler at Hotel Limatambo so, instead of being an observer, as I had hoped, I was now among the cast and crew. The tension began to build as we reached San Mateo, at about 11,000 feet. Indian women in bright shawls who boarded the coach to sell snacks of meat and cheese did not seem surprised when most of the passengers refused. Conversation was noticeably subdued as we pulled away, rocking and jolting toward Ticlio, an ascent of nearly 5,000 feet.

An Indio woman behind me was the first to fold. Then her infant child became sick. Watching them, a teenager a few seats away turned pale, then bolted toward the toilet, but there were several people in line ahead of him. Outside it was cold, but everyone was hurrying to open their windows. Out of nowhere, a man appeared with a mop and bucket and a woman in a white smock began attending to the sick, making trips with a green bladder filled with oxygen. The bladder smelled like an old football and I winced every time she passed by. My seating partner was Luis Campuzano, a pleasant man who bore an astonishing resemblance to Sammy Davis and was a born-again Christian. He had asked to borrow one of my magazines; then, after nearly two hours of silence, he endeared himself to me by abruptly inquiring if Frank Sinatra was still alive and was I, by chance, related to John Wayne?

Just outside Ticlio, I asked Luis how he was feeling. He spoke almost no English, which made his careful selection of words even more impressive. "Like the dog poop, that is how," Luis said.

I wasn't tip-top myself. My joints ached, my head hurt, and I felt like tripping that woman with the green bladder. At 16,000 feet, the air is bitter, like ice on the lungs; the brain, numb from sending out drowning signals, goes into survival mode. The bitch had only herself to blame if she swung that thing past my nose one more time.

It was dark as we began our descent toward Mantaro Valley and Huancayo beyond. My stomach rallied and Luis looked on in unmasked admiration as I ate a big dinner of rice and some kind of meat. But my brain was still up there at Ticlio, feeling mean. Two British guys sitting across from the sick Indio woman were smoking cigarettes. The woman was making a show of trying to fan the smoke away from her child's face, the poor thing looking gaunt and miserable with huge glassy eyes. Other than myself, the two Brits were the only English-speaking people on the coach, and I began to feel some insane complicity. We'd saved their asses at Normandy, and now these two had the gall to implicate me with their rude behavior.

"Hey," I told the closest one, "That baby's *sick*."

"So?"

"So the smoke's bothering them. Put out your cigarettes."

"She hasn't said anything to us."

"Babies can't talk, you *dolt*."

"The baby's mother, I mean—"

I stood up. Maybe they could see that I was altitude crazy, for I surely was. Behind me, Luis was tapping two Uzi-carrying policemen on the arm, pointing and saying, "Senior Wayne, si? Es genuino." The policemen were grinning and later would ask to have their photographs taken with me.

The British guys put out their cigarettes.

O O O

In fairness to Peru, it is unlikely that my last day in Huancayo is representative of what tour literature calls "the common travel experience." I was up at first light and out on the streets, roaming that section of alleys where the Indians cook their morning meals before going to work. Huancayo is a drab city of 85,000 people and, aside from a Sunday fair that attracts artisans from the surrounding mountains, it offers little in the way of color, so I looked forward to this walk among the Indians. I stopped at a stand where a woman was cooking over a propane stove and asked if I might buy a breakfast. She sent her son running for coffee, then ladled out soup and set the bowl before me. There was a jawbone in the bowl, complete with teeth; goat teeth, it turned out—a startling thing to face early in the morning, but the soup was good.

As I was eating, a noise from behind caught my attention, and I turned to see two men scratching and punching at each other, while a third man waved a revolver in the air, trying to draw a bead on one of them. The man with the gun wore a nice pink sweater; the other two were dressed in rags. When things calmed down a little, I poked my camera under my arm and tried to get a picture of them; for reasons I couldn't understand, this terrified the woman who had served me soup. She came hurrying toward me, whispering anxiously in Quechua. I understood none of it, but still got the clear impression that if the man in the pink sweater caught me taking his picture, the revolver might be aimed my way. Perhaps he was a member of the Peruvian Secret Police; I never found out.

The woman called to her son again, a boy of about ten, who took me cheerfully by the elbow and began to steer me down the street. The boy's name was Edwin, and he held my elbow all the way back to the hotel. Edwin smiled a lot and talked. I have no idea what he said. He wore a hooded serape and his toes stuck out of a hole in one shoe. He waved at people and called the local dogs by name. I liked Edwin, and it was heartbreaking to think he lived on streets where men in sweaters waved revolvers at men who wore rags. As I stood in the lobby of the hotel, Edwin walked backward so that he could wave to me. He waved for an entire block.

That afternoon, I paid a guide from Foptur (a Peruvian touring agency) to take me to a place where I could fly cast for trout. We drove for two hours over bad roads and ended up at a country restaurant where outdoor tables surrounded a tiny pond. The guide, whose name was Marybel, led me to the pond's edge and pointed. "See? Theese is the trout," she said as if by way of introduction.

Yes, I could see the trout, but she surely didn't mean I was to fish here? There were people at the tables lunching who, if snagged by my back cast, might retaliate with some kind of unpleasantness.

She considered the problem as if surprised. Yes, I was right. In that case, perhaps I could just buy her dinner?

By the time we got back to Huancayo, it was dark. I had decided en route to seek out Edwin and his mother again, for I wasn't altogether sure I'd paid for the soup, plus I wanted to give Edwin more money. Peruvian currency, the inti, looks like Monopoly money (and is worth just about the same on the international exchange), so one generally underpays out of confusion. Edwin, I felt, deserved more for his kindness.

Outside the hotel, the Municipal Plaza was crowded with people celebrating the city's 416th anniversary. A folk band was playing, flutes and a guitar. As I stopped to listen, two college-age guys brushed by me. One of them stopped, studied me for a moment, then spit on my shoes. I looked in his eyes. Had he meant to do that? Yes, he'd meant to do that.

As they swaggered off, I turned and walked back past the hotel and down the street toward the alley where I had seen Edwin that morning. As I walked, I heard footsteps behind me and glanced over my shoulder to see the silhouettes of two men. They seemed thicker, taller than the college guys, but I couldn't be sure. The streets were empty here, and the sidewalk was elevated about three feet off the pavement. The men were getting closer, but I paid them no attention. They were in a hurry and I was not. Suddenly, something hit me in the back with a tremendous impact and drove me forward. I would have fallen, but there was some kind of sign or railing that I caught with my right hand. In a panic, I swung around blindly and my left fist hit something solid. Now the two men were in the street, one sitting on the pavement, the other on one knee. What were they doing there?

"You guys got a problem?"—I yelled the question, as if yelling might help them translate. I was scared and in shock, and I'll never forget the way they looked at me; a weird animal look, like dazed dogs.

I was already backing away, ready to run as they got quickly to their feet. But instead of attacking me again, they hurried off in the direction I had been walking. I jogged the other way, back to the hotel. When I got into my room, I took off my vest—one of those travel vests with a lot of pockets. My knuckle was split, seeping blood, and as I was looking around for something to clean it, I noticed that the big pocket in the back of the vest was slit. I took out the thick notebook I kept there. It was slit too. I opened the notebook and saw that a stab mark penetrated about a quarter of an inch into the sheets. It took a long, dull moment for me to finally understand what had happened: The bastards had stabbed me; just walked up and stabbed me without a word of warning. The knife had slit the notebook and the vest when I swung around.

Now I was shaking. I was furious. If the notebook hadn't been in the vest's back pocket, the knife would have gone into my kidney. That's why they had looked at me with such weird expressions—they couldn't figure out why I wasn't hurt.

I dropped the vest on the floor, feeling sick and sad and dirty; I wanted to take them both by the throat and squeeze until their eyes turned the color of muscat grapes.

I took off my clothes and went into the bathroom.

It was 6:50 p.m.

○ ○ ○

The terrorist attack lasted nearly four hours, and I counted 12 explosions close enough to shake the walls of the hotel. At what seemed the peak of the battle, I returned upstairs to find that Siskel and Ebert had abandoned their chairs to two nurses from Lima. The nurses were drinking wine and said they wanted to practice their English. It would keep their minds off the bombs, they said. I watched the police lights on the plaza as one of the nurses rattled on about how they were in Huancayo with a medical convention and one of the neurosurgeons was trying to get them in bed, so they were avoiding him, and would I mind staying, because then he wouldn't come around.

The gunfire was sporadic but very close, and I was thinking the police shouldn't be using the rotating strobes on their cars. It made them easy targets, which was just too stupid for words.

One of the nurses was asking me things, I can't remember what, and then she wanted to look at my hand—she had something in her room that could take care of *that*—and I watched, during a series of rapid rifle shots, as one of the police cars stopped abruptly and three officers jumped out.

The nurse was saying that her room was next to mine—"Isn't that a thing that is funny?"—as one of the officers was illuminated briefly in a blue wedge of strobe and, in that same instant, jolted backwards as a rifle shot popped. Now I could see his feet kicking wildly with every revolution of the light. "We are the neighbors," said the nurse.

I told the nurses that a man had just been shot down there, and they said, yes, weren't things terrible in the mountains and, if they had known, they would never have come. This sort of thing did not happen in Lima, they said. Lima was different.

○ ○ ○

Marybel, the driver from Foptur, took me to the train station the next morning. She seemed nervous; the bombs had kept her awake, she told me. She had heard on the local radio that many of the street people, the Indios, had been injured or killed, but she knew no details. No, she said, Sendero had never attacked Huancayo before (a lie); no, the police were not allowing vehicles into the portion of town where the Indians cooked (another lie) and, besides, the chances of finding one little boy in such a short time were not good (the truth).

The trip back to Lima took 13 hours. En route, the train stopped unexpectedly at a place where there was no village, and we sat and sat and, finally, I got out to take a look. The engine was gone; it just disappeared and no one knew why. I took a seat on the trestle, which overlooked the narrow road that led from Huancayo to Lima. While there, I spoke with Jeff McClelland, the only American I met while in Peru. McClelland, from Georgia, had been traveling the country for eight months and he told me that he, too, had been attacked in Huancayo. Five men had knocked him down and taken his money, his shirt, his belt, and his shoes. But it was his own fault, McClelland said, because he had been drunk and should not have been on the streets alone—the curious reaction of every traveling American I've ever met who has been wronged in a foreign country; as if some inherent national guilt excuses any offense.

I told McClelland that if the engine didn't return to the train shortly (we had already been there two hours), I was going to walk down to the road and hitchhike into Lima. He said he didn't think it was a good idea. Americans shouldn't hitchhike in Peru, he told me, then added ruefully, "I love this country, but I've learned to hate it, too. Life means almost nothing here."

Within the week, an American agronomist, Constantine Orson Gregory, would drive down that same stretch of road, only to be stopped by Sendero. The Senderistas would pull Gregory and his companion out of their truck, make them kneel, then shoot them both in the back of the head. Gregory was 25 years old.

My last day in Lima, I read about the attack on Huancayo in the newspaper *La Republica*. It said four policemen had been wounded and 30 suspects arrested in "the night of terror." The story made no mention of civilian casualties and was written in the same florid prose that, in Peru, is usually reserved for earthquakes, flash floods, and similar acts of God.

To Say the Tiger's Name

Each dusk during our raft trip down Sumatra's Alas River, Rossman, the Malayan guide, would light seven candles and place them around the perimeter of our camp—a liturgical touch complemented by neither the surroundings nor our recent behavior.

Rossman finally told me, "It is to keep *her* away," not because he wanted to tell me, but because I pressed him, following him around as he positioned the small flames, this brown man with his straw hat, splayed feet, and missing teeth.

Her?

"Her. Nenek." He was grinning and shaking his head. "Naw, naw, I won't say her name."

Whose name? Nenek? He had just said it—Nenek.

"Naw, naw. I don't say *her* name."

David Heckman, director of Sobek Expedition's Sumatra base, heard him and chided, "Come on, Rossman, tell him the name. You're a modern man, now. You can say it."

Rossman was still shaking his head, smiling, and he winced slightly as Heckman began to explain, "He lights those candles to keep tigers away. The Malay word for tiger is *hari mau,* but no one says it—not in the jungle, anyway. Instead, they use 'Nenek,' a replacement word; kind of a euphemism. It's an old taboo, for to say the tiger's name is to call the tiger. Call the tiger, and the tiger will always come."

No tigers came that night. I know—I was awake and listening. I kept my boots on too, in case someone had to get to the raft and untie it real fast. In the morning, the jungle crowded in, a gloom of gigantic leaves and dark shapes blurred by fog and tendrils of low cloud. There was no sun, and the only soure of light seemed to be the river, a liquescent split in the mountains mirrored by a streak of sky.

Heckman and Rossman were taking me down the Alas to give me an idea of what Sobek's Sumatran operation is like. Sobek is a California-based company that specializes in international adventure packages, and it has been operating in Sumatra since 1984. Heckman, who came in 1985, knows the country well, and he told me before we started that the best part of the river was where it was sided by national park on one bank and national preserve on the other—the section we were now about to enter.

We packed our gear into the raft, and the river carried us along at about seven knots into the expanding hills. Three helmeted hornbills flushed before us: huge birds with grotesque heads, their wings creaking as if on bad hinges. A family of macaques watched us pass, the largest male looking like an evil little man, peering out from the high limbs of a kampur tree. The forest continued to close in, absorbing sounds, a transforming light, then Heckman suddenly motioned for Rossman to steer us toward shore. "Listen!" he said. "Hear that? Those are apes; black gibbons!"

I listened; then I could do nothing but listen. There was a high, wild honk, then howls on a descending scale; the howls of something that seemed more human than animal, and they went right to the heart. One solitary call echoed from the forest, then was answered by another, and yet another, until dozens of gibbons were all calling at once. Yet the forest was motionless; mist was still in the high canopy, and it was as if the sound originated from the trees themselves. We sat and listened for nearly half an hour, until the gibbons had finished their morning display. I taped most of it, for I have never heard any sound that better characterizes the essential nature of rain forest; the primal source.

It's one of those tapes I hope I somehow manage not to lose—for a sound we heard within minutes of pulling away from that bank is much more common in Sumatra, and the tape may soon be irreplaceable. The new sound was a high mechanical whine, like dirt bikes racing. The river carried us inexorably closer to it—a puzzling noise to me—and as we passed beneath a high cliff, the forest seemed to explode above us. At the oars, Rossman panicked momentarily, rowing furiously, for the noise of the explosion was sustained and coming toward us, growing louder. Something was crashing through the trees a hundred feet above us, about to tumble off the cliff. Dust and leaves were raining down on the water; Rossman was still rowing for all our lives, and I sat there thinking, *Geeze, I survive a tiger taboo only to be squashed by a rock slide.*

But then the crashing noise ceased, and all was silent again save for the same mechanical whine, which was now much louder. Finally, I realized what the noise was; what had happened. Heckman certainly knew, for he had made this trip many times. But all he said was, "That's the sound of the modern forest. That's the sound of modern Sumatra."

Above us, Sumatra's national preserve was being logged with chain saws.

○ ○ ○

The only thing modern about Sumatra is its problems. Consider its largest city, Medan. You fly in over mangrove plains off the Strait of Malacca to see a plateau of orange smog as vivid as the hot haze of a chemical fire. The smog seems to lie over jungle—a strata of red gas over shimmering green—but then the jungle thins, becomes veined with dirt roads, patched with rice paddies, and the horizon swells into a coagulated gray mass of slums, television antennas, and frantic traffic: Welcome to the second largest island in the nation of Indonesia (Borneo is larger) and the fifth largest island in the world.

More than a million people reside in Medan, and there seem to be at least that many beat-up minibuses and motorized rickshaws. Few of the vehicles have mufflers, but they all have horns, and the narrow streets are a smoking, squealing lunacy that link the open markets, filthy restaurants, sleazy bars, teenage prostitutes, swaggering cops, women cooking over wood fires, sleeping drunks, pretty children flirting from doorways, and the few stray dogs that have not been eaten. "Imagine a completely lawless, immoral place where everyone wants to have fun and almost no one wants to work—that's Medan," Heckman told me upon my arrival. Later, during the long bus trip through the mountains to the headwaters of the Alas, he would use almost the same words to define Sumatra itself. It was nearly 3 a.m.; the narrow switchbacks provided a vehicular drama not conducive to sleep, plus there seemed to be an inordinate amount of traffic for one-lane mountain roads at such an hour. I began to take note. In the space of 30 minutes, we met a dozen heavy trucks. The cargo of each truck was covered with a tarp, but no tarp can disguise the shape of raw timber. Another half hour passed in which I counted 15 more trucks, all loaded and covered.

Heckman stirred in the seat ahead of me, and I told him what I had seen.

"This is the only road out of the national park, right?" He nodded.

I pressed: "That's why they're shipping the timber out at night—because it's illegal. But the Indonesian government has to be aware of what's going on. I mean, this is no small operation."

Heckman said he'd better not comment for publication—he liked living in Sumatra, and Sobek wanted to maintain its base there. He didn't want the Indonesian government angry at him. "That's not the way you change things here," he said. It was then he defined Sumatra with the same words he had used to define Medan.

What is going on in Sumatra is, of course, going on in impoverished countries all over the world. When stray dogs become a part of the citizenry's menu, speeches about the long-term benefits of virgin rain forest won't turn a single head—never mind the sympathies of corrupt governments. But it's especially tragic on an island that still has the richest list of fauna in Indonesia: gibbons, leaf monkeys, macaques, elephants, Sumatran tigers, clouded leopards, Sumatran rhinos. And it is one of only two places in the world where the orangutan is found. But Indonesia, goaded by the Japanese yen, continues cutting its forests faster than any nation on earth, and Sumatra continues to produce about 80 percent of that timber—a billion-dollar-a-year industry on an island where the average adult male earns less than $1 a day, and where payoffs and political corruption are part of the national fabric.

In such a place, denotations such as "national park" and "national preserve" are euphemisms meaningful only in that they mark regions where the bulldozers have not reached, but soon will.

○ ○ ○

We spent two more days on the Alas River, but neither compared with those 30 minutes listening to the black gibbons. Our last night, we camped on a sandbar above the village of Gelombang—one of those plywood and tarpaper slums thrown up by a lumber company for its workers. In the morning, a boy in a dugout canoe came paddling frantically toward our tents, yelling, "Nenek! Nenek!" for he had just found fresh tracks a few hundred yards down river from our camp.

Rossman nodded, not at all surprised, for he already knew what Indonesia has yet to understand. If you call the tiger, the tiger will surely come.

—

Jumping with the
Polar Bears

—

*Cabin fever: 1. A cerebral itch, exacerbated by deep
snow and bad craziness, which penicillin can't cure but
tickets to Maui and a new roommate might.*

—R.W.W.

laskans cannot be credited with inventing bizarre behavior,
though their claims of elevating it to an art form must be
taken seriously.

Consider the snow crazed who travel to the port town of Seward
each January to swim in Resurrection Bay. Consider the thousands
who come to watch them. Consider the—hell, consider just about
anyone who has endured a winter north of Juneau. You can spot
them on the sidewalk. They stand out from the laity like exhibits in a

van Gogh retrospective. Real snow vets have a look in their eye; a glow of crazy wisdom. The wisdom is infectious. It knows no strangers and welcomes all life forms—especially in winter. Which is why I consider visiting Alaska in January one of the best travel decisions I have ever made.

An example: At 3 a.m. on my first morning in Anchorage, jet-lagged and hungry and unable to sleep, I looked down from a tenth-floor hotel window to see what appeared to be two men playing tennis in the middle of the street. I say "appeared to be" because a howling snowstorm seriously compromises visibility.

I pressed my face to the window: Yes, they were playing tennis all right. No mistaking those wicked passing shots.

But were they really using showshoes for rackets?

Well, that's what it looked like: two beer sops gliding around an icy street using snowshoes to knock a ball over an imaginary net.

Perfect, I thought, already reaching for my clothes—athletes this enterprising would certainly know where to find food at 3 a.m.

I have an unfailing instinct for such things, which is why, 30 minutes later, over sourdough waffles and reindeer sausage, one of the players patiently explained why they had volunteered to lead me to this all-night restaurant.

"Because we could tell you're new to Alaska."

"Oh?"

"You got tan ears. Plus, wearing those socks for mittens."

"Ah-h-h-h."

"Yeah. And, nobody who knew anything about Alaska woulda asked if we were hitting the ball with snowshoes. Snowshoes are too valuable. And they're too big. That'd just look weird."

Tennis in a 3 a.m. blizzard was no time to risk the illusion of odd behavior, I quickly agreed.

"Exactly," said one of my new friends. "We're like anybody else. Nights we can't sleep, we just feel like getting out and hitting a few balls on the ice. Maybe shoot our guns a little. Maybe kill something. You know, come to town and shake off the cabin fever."

It all seemed so reasonable, once explained.

Having spent most of my life in the South, I had no experience with cabin fever. But I instantly perceived that cabin fever and crazy wisdom were inexorably linked. Understanding the affliction, I decided, would be an important step in understanding Alaska. It might also shed light on why, in an instant of madness, I had agreed to travel to Seward and dive into Resurrection Bay with a lot of peole who, unlike me, had a built-in excuse for aberrant behavior: Being Alaskans, aberrant behavior was not only accepted, it was encouraged.

I visited Anchorage book stores, but didn't find a good definition of the malady. I met with Linda Billington, a long-time Alaska resident and a writer for the Anchorage *Daily News,* who suggested I construct my own definition from interviews with fever sufferers. "But don't expect to get all the information you need here," she laughed. "You know what they say: The best thing about Anchorage is that it's so close to Alaska."

Even so, I immediately began collecting data; interviewing patrons of well-known bars such as Chilkoot Charlie's and The Bird House, an old trapper's line cabin that has cheered more than one victim of snow madness. Every Alaskan has a favorite cabin fever story, and distilling the key elements into aphorism is no easy task, even though the threads are darned interesting: broken hearts, broken spirits, broken dishes, broken noses, and a thing called a Spenard Divorce, which is an Alaskan euphemism for putting a bullet through one's beloved.

Not one person mentioned swimming in Resurrection Bay in January.

Seward's infamous Polar Bear Jump-off, I was to learn, is not for the cabin feverish. It is for the seriously cabin twisted.

Batfishing in the Rainforest

Cabin fever: 2. Disease resulting from a caged
imagination that has equal access to maps of the
lower 48 states and to the 44-caliber Smith & Wesson
in the upper cupboard.

—R.W.W.

One could spend an entire summer planning a winter trip to Alaska because winter in Alaska is just one damn fun event after another.

That's the way some Alaskans put it: "one damn fun thing after another," for they are a poetic people.

There's the Athabascan Fiddling Festival (Fairbanks), the Anchorage Symphony of Trees, the Russian Orthodox Christmas (Kodiak and Sitka), and a long list of dogsled races, ice-climbing events, and snow-machine rallies.

Some of the events suggest feverish antecedents: the Cordova Ice Worm Festival, the Heart Throb Biathlon (Nome), the Nenana Banana Eating and Tripod Raising Contest (Nenana), the Bering Sea Ice Golf Classic (orange golf balls recommended; hand tools allowed).

"One thing about Alaskans," Celeste Dorsey tells me, "we know how to make our own fun."

They also know how to drive on ice—which is why I have opted, on this trip from Anchorage to Seward, to beg a ride from Celeste rather than risk the 120 miles of snow-packed highway on my own.

It is not difficult begging a ride in Alaska. Indeed, Alaskans are so unfailingly friendly that one suspects long isolation and inbreeding have produced a kinder, more fun-loving subspecies of American— either that, or heavy exposure to "Gilligan's Island" reruns has imprinted in them an enthusiasm for visitors. Whatever the reason, it is a refreshing thing to walk the sidewalks of a major city (Anchorage) and receive greetings from strangers. After only a day in that city, I had the strong impression, correct or not, that I could have asked anyone for assistance and it would have been provided in full measure.

Celeste is a good choice as a driver, though, for at least two reasons: She is field director of the American Cancer Society, which sponsors the Polar Bear Jump-off, so she can tell me about the event's history. Also, her car has studded tires, and Celeste assures me that she knows how to use them.

We leave in weather that is typical for southern Alaska in January: a screaming sleet storm that twice changes from rain to hail before settling into a full-blown blizzard as we reach the foothills of the Chugach Mountains.

"Ought to be nice and warm for your swim," Celeste observes cheerily. "Two years ago, it was 37 below. Tomorrow might even get up to freezing."

I am so numbed by the white-out driving conditions on this curving mountain road that I can hardly reply to her comments about the weather. But Celeste chats on: "Just so long as it doesn't get too warm. The Seward polar plunge is the world's coldest swim; most folks like it that way."

The world's coldest swim—that much I already knew. And Celeste has kindly filled in the remaining blanks: The Seward Jump-off began six winters ago when, to raise money for the Cancer Society, a tiny group of Sewardites (a name they relish) secured backers who would pay the association hard cash if the fund-raisers really did jump in the bay.

The fund-raisers jumped; the backers paid; a new Alaskan tradition was founded.

Celeste tells me, "Those first years, we didn't have very many jumpers. But it's really taken off in the last two or three years. Now Seward runs a week-long festival in conjunction with the jump. They have ice bowling, a bachelor auction, a dog weight-pulling contest, a chili feed—all kinds of stuff. Even so, in the six years combined, we have had fewer than a hundred jumpers."

I am surprised there have been so few—and take time out from gripping the dashboard to say so.

Celeste explains, "Thousands have come to watch but, let's face it: How many people are actually crazy enough to jump into the Gulf of Alaska in January? We'll have 24 or 25 jumpers this year, the most ever, and it keeps getting bigger and bigger. People from the lower 48 are already contacting us about signing up for next year. It's getting to be like a prestige thing to say you've done the world's coldest swim; that you're a Seward Polar Bear. And it should be. We call our jumpers, 'the few, the brave, the frozen.'"

We have been on the road for more than three hours, in which time I have seen nothing but a dizzying thatchwork of headlights, snow, and a suggestive gray vacuum that, I am certain, marks a precipice and horrible death if Celeste continues to drift these damn curves.

Even so, her words stir me: the few, the brave—the *frozen*.

Forty-eight hours ago, I had never even met a cabin fever victim. But after tomorrow's jump, I can walk into any bar in Alaska and hold my head up proudly—for I will be one of them.

Cabin fever: 3. Emotional turmoil that occurs when four damn walls have interfered once too often with three or more essential vices: i.e., beer swilling, sunbathing, and fornication for purposes other than survival.

—R.W.W.

Because of the blizzard, it is morning before I get my first look at Seward. Late morning, actually, because, in these northern climes, it is dark by 4:30 p.m. and does not get light again until nearly 10 a.m. I step outside and look over my shoulder to see that I have slept at the Van Gilder Hotel, a classy raspberry-colored relic from Alaska's hinterland days. Before me is the city of Seward (population 3,000), a grid of brick buildings and New England–style homes; a pretty little city that has a rugged frontier light.

What really stops me, though, is the backdrop. Seward sits on the edge of a great body of water, Resurrection Bay, in a basin created by snow peaks. All around me, there are mountains. The mountains are the bruised blue of thunderheads; the bay, misted by a driving wind, is gray. Through the mist, the mountains rise as abruptly as glaciers, creating the illusion of motion, an illusion that produces a brooding sense of impermanence. Looking at those drifting mountains, I feel as if I am a miniature person standing on the toy sidewalk of a miniature town.

Alaska does that to visitors. At a stroke, it elevates and numbs. One's first look can be so overwhelming that the mind balks. In every direction, it seems, is a new photograph from an expensive outdoor calendar. That's the way the mind deals with it: *Transmissions from the eye can't be valid.* Alaska is simply too beautiful, too spacious, too . . . energized to be assimilated at a glance, let alone believed. To come to grips with the beauty of Alaska, I think, a person would have to live here long enough to become indifferent to the landscape and then, slowly, from that indifference, reassemble bits and scraps of scenery until, finally, the beauty would seem believable.

But I have been in Seward only a few hours, so I move dumbly through the streets. In the next couple of days, I will come to know many of the people who now nod and smile at me. I will ride in their cars and eat in their homes. We will attend the bachelorette auction and the fish fry and sled dog pull. We will share stories and laugh a lot. Now, though, I walk alone—or, I should say, slide alone, for the streets are great slabs of ice. Every block, it seems, I come perilously close to falling because I am clumsy under the best of circumstances, but a thoroughly dangerous man when on a skid.

At Resurrection Bay, I stand and watch a sea otter swim by—then almost fall. At the frozen Little League diamond, I nearly fall as I turn to watch a half dozen bald eagles sitting in a tree. Which is bad enough, but there are plenty of people around to see. The Polar Bear Parade will soon start, and streets are busy with the strange commerce of decorated pickup trucks, high school cheerleaders, and people in weird costumes. It is a tradition for those who jump in the bay to wear bizarre costumes. (According to Celeste, caped super heros are popular, but so are giant beer cans—which are also metaphorically more in tune with the event.) Yet these people, even though they are extravagantly dressed, move over the ice with ease, if not grace.

I don't mind the pain of falling. It's the indignity I'd like to avoid. I am already shamefully underdressed—I have come all the way from Florida to jump, but have brought no costume. To fall now, with my fellow jumpers looking on—King Neptune, Moose Man, Leopard Lady, Mr. Gorilla, and the rest—would be to invite additional disgrace.

With the exaggerated care of a palsied hemorrhoid sufferer, I make my way across the ice and take my place in the parade body. Soon the parade begins to slide amoeba-like toward the small boat basin.

I expect the street to get better. It does not. Our route follows an ice sheen that seems to go on forever. There is absolutely no footing.

"How far do we have to march?" I ask Leopard Lady. Those of us who will jump have gravitated into a tight group; a brotherhood of fools walking shoulder to shoulder.

"About a mile," Leopard Lady tells me, unconcerned. And why should she be? She isn't sliding. Nor are the others. (Later, Flip Foldger of the local hardware store would share a local secret—wood screws in the boot soles.) But now, for me, this isn't a parade; it's proof that hell does freeze over.

Oh, Lordy, I grieve silently, *will these damn trials never end?*
But I endure.

Finally, we reach the small boat basin with its restaurant and boardwalk and docks with rows of moored boats. There are people everywhere; throngs of people pressed up against the shoreline to salute us few who are about to throw ourselves into the bay.

Out of the blue, King Neptune says to me, "I guess the ambulance is here because of that guy last year. Guy got out of the water and couldn't stop shaking. He had to be hospitalized."

Truthfully, I haven't thought much about the swim. I have taken cold showers, so I know about cold water, right?

Now I'm not so sure. King Neptune is correct—the ambulance is sitting right there by the dock. And the water of Resurrection Bay is unlike any water I've ever showered in: It's gray in color, but crystal clear, like a great slab of smoky quartz. Also, there is ice floating in it. Not just chunks, but great slushy pools, as if a 7-11 barge has gone aground and suffered a Big Gulp spill. Saltwater, I know, freezes at about 29 degrees F so, yeah, this is probably colder than the kind of showers I'm used to.

From the harbor patrol boat, the announcer begins to call jumpers. One by one they go: Leopard Lady, Moose Man, Happy Hooker, Moth Woman, and the rest. They jump feet first and immediately thrash their way to the surface, hands flailing, eyes wild.

I begin to feel better.

The shock hasn't killed anyone outright. Plus, let's face it, I'm not only a professional outdoorsman, I am a professional *waterman*. These people may be ballerinas on ice, but the water is my turf. It's time, I decide, to give these cabin fever sufferers a little taste of sea school, mano a mano.

By the time the announcer calls my name, I have already stripped down to my jogging shorts and approach the dock with a well-formulated plan in mind: I will dive in headfirst, then surface with an Esther Williams flourish. I once interviewed Ms. Williams, and feel I know exactly how she would handle this situation: toes pointed, back arched, while finger-splashing a poetic water-lace out onto the adoring crowd. Nothing heavy or obvious; just a joyous reminder that not everyone in the world swims like a foundered dog.

I step onto the dock and leap into the air with toes pointed . . . and the next thing I remember is the unpleasant sensation of the crowd hooting because I have lost my shorts. I'd pull my shorts up, but I cannot move because my fingers are numb on arms that will not work. Parts of me are retracting farther and more boldly than at any time in my life, and I would yell for help, but my mind has gone dead.

Later, I will do the research I should have done prior to the jump, and I will learn of the physiological hysteria that started the instant my face hit the water. First, there's a thing called the vagal nerve response, which has to do with the pneumogastric or tenth cranial nerve. If one dives headfirst into near-freezing water, this bastard gears down like a busted Yamaha and, for reasons I still don't understand, nearly stops the heart. At the same instant, a phenomenon known as the mammalian dive reflex takes control, shunting blood from the body's extremities to the vital organs, rendering one about as agile as a hibernating bear.

Actually, I am lucky that I can move at all. About 10 percent of people who are suddenly submerged in cold water can't—and so they sink.

I don't sink, but neither can I swim. Fighting my way to the surface is like trying to dog-paddle through cold ether. But somehow, some way, I reach out and grab the dock. Then I make it to a blanket . . . then to my clothes . . . then to one of Seward's 13 bars where, with fellow members of the elite Seward Polar Bear Club, we celebrate the fever in us that has now been cured.

Batfishing in the
Rainforest

Despite heavy rain, fruit bats were hitting on yellow poppers, those Styrofoam lures some people learn how to make by reading fly-fishing magazines. Rudy Dodero, an excellent caster, would haul the popper off the water, shoot line into the jungle darkness, shoot again on the fore cast, and let the popper swing into the lights of the dock where the river current boiled in an oleaginous slick.

"See? Es coming now, man. I strip eet in slow, real slooow, make it splash. See 'em? Hear them fruit bats pooping?"

Peeping; that's what I think Rudy meant.

Into the annulated haze came these shadowy creatures, little rats on wings vectoring wildly toward the lure. I ducked, reasoning that fruit bats may not be attracted to artificials, but vampire bats might be. (Actually, they were probably *Noctilio leporinus,* the fish-eating bats of Central America—not that I would have recognized a fish-eating bat had I landed one.)

There was a grunt, a moment of mad thrashing, and I looked up to see Dodero, one of the most knowledgeable fly-fishermen in all of Costa Rica, silhouetted by dock lights against a scrim of silver rain, back arched, rod bowed, smiling as his line flew heavenward—an inspiring sight.

This was at Río Colorado Lodge on the Caribbean coast of Costa Rica, a comfortable outpost 14 miles from the Nicaraguan border. Río Colorado is considered by many to offer the best tarpon and snook fishing in the world—something that one who's made his living as a fishing guide in Florida for the last nine years should not admit. The lodge is located on a river that flows from the jungle right into the Caribbean. No roads, no towns, no barrier islands, just this river and a bunch of lagoons making a straight shot into the sea; a confluence of wilderness water to which predatory fish come unimpeded, ready to feed. If you want to be certain of catching a large fish on fly rod, then you book the three-day package at Río Colorado Lodge ($745 for double occupancy: rooms, meals, drinks, guide, and in-country travel all included).

I did not come to Costa Rica to catch tarpon (a jumping fish that commonly weighs more than a hundred pounds and looks like a giant chrome-glazed herring) or snook (a smaller game fish, wedge-headed, with a black lateral stripe like something dreamed up in Detroit), so I had not booked the three-day package. I had come to Costa Rica specifically to fish for Pacific sailfish on fly rod; in fact, planned to try and beat the world record, the one held by Stu Apte, the famous fly-fisherman who in 1965 landed a 136-pound Pacific sail on 12-pound tippet. That I had found my way to the Caribbean coast, where there are no Pacific sailfish, and that I was now standing in the rain watching the manager of Río Colorado Lodge play a flying reptile, were, I suppose, illustrative not only of Costa Rica's charm but also of the peculiar lunacy that embraces one just beyond the portals of many exacting sports.

"Reptile?" said Dodero looking over his shoulder, the fly line still describing high, wild patterns. "Where you learn that crazy thing? Bat es no reptile, man."

Oh.

This was in May, right on the front edge of Costa Rica's rainy season. The rainy season, which lasts through November, is not considered the ideal time to tour a country in Central America, but it happens to be when the fishing in Costa Rica—always good—is at its very best. Why this was of concern to me, why fishing is still the nucleus around which I plan every trip, mystifies my friends almost as much as it continues to mystify me. In late April I had celebrated my 1,800th career fishing charter by attending taco night at a bar on Sanibel Island, and before leaving for Costa Rica, had guided more than a hundred trips during a four-month period, a withering schedule of being on the docks before light and finishing at the cleaning table just before dark. It is this marathon of wind and water, plus the Florida tourist rush, that produces in the operators of fishing vessels a phenomenon known as Twig Syndrome, or Guides' Disease, a psychological distemper with a whole bunch of unattractive symptoms: Snapping like a dry twig is one, and maybe leaving your boat to go on a fishing vacation is another. Now I was witnessing a couple of new symptoms, I thought, watching Dodero out there in the rain, grinning into the darkness. The poor guy had a case of it himself—and no wonder, holed up 12 months a year with a beautiful wife and a wonderful son in this paradise of rain forest and wild monkeys, dealing with interesting people and fishing every day.

"Nice-looking bat, Rudy."

"Sí. Not so bad, huh?" He loosened the drag abruptly, giving slack, then watched as the creature dropped the hook, fluttered for a moment, and banked off toward wherever it is Central American bats go after having the bejesus surprised out of them. "Clean release. Nice an' clean. He's a happy theeng, no? Happy to be free." Dodero was reeling in the line now, making the lure splash in transport, and I looked on in mild fear that something else would swoop down out of the sky and eat it.

"Yeah, Rudy, that's one happy bat."

"Es not a reptile, though. Bat es a mammal, man." He was checking the lure, clicking his tongue at the fang marks, saying as he did, "You want to catch reptiles, turtles and snakes 'n' theengs, you got to use streamer flies. White es good; sometimes red. Not poppers, though; reptiles won't hit poppers. 'Cept for frogs, maybe."

Oh.

Fun and beauty exact their toll.

○ ○ ○

There may be ulterior motives intertwined in this passion of mine for fishing distant lands. Judge for yourself.

Understand first that a rod strapped to your back serves as more than just a device by which you can yank unfamiliar fish from unfamiliar waters. As a stranger without motive in a strange place, your presence is often viewed with mistrust if not outright suspicion. Carry a fishing rod, though, and people who normally wouldn't stop to give you directions will drop everything to give detailed misinformation and lie about the local angling. Women will sometimes even offer food, assuming—too often correctly—that you haven't caught anything and probably won't. Also, I always choose a country where the fishing is supposed to be superb, yet has enough local character so that the fishing really doesn't matter so much once you get there. I settle upon a place I would like to see, then spend evenings after my charters with books and maps, doing research while I tie the prescribed flies beneath the reading light in my office. This is called armchair fishing, a fantasy sport discouragingly more productive than the real thing. Before leaving for Costa Rica, I had tied and packaged 40 leaders and 40 big streamer flies, rehearsing this scene as I did: Me on the stern of a boat, a record-shattering sailfish at my feet, hands blistered, sweat pouring, blithely waving away the crew's appeals that I rest, yelling up to the fly bridge, "Swing her around for another pass, Julio! Might as well break the world record on eight-pound while we're out here." Silly stuff like that.

But the passion to fish often begins to ebb shortly after arrival, usually at a speed directly influenced by the number of other things there are to do. Beer and hammocks sometimes play a role too. Remember that I usually take these trips immediately after the spring charter marathon: a time when Twig Syndrome is in full blossom, and the pressure to put fish in the boat has rendered even the best of fishing guides a jelly blob of neuroses and bad language. In the grip of this malady I once went to Little Cayman Island to fish for bonefish on fly, but ended up doing a bird count. I went to Belize to fish for permit, but spent most of my time in the back of a pickup, happily riding through the rain forests of Guatemala. I went to Cuba to fish for anything, but ended up scuba diving twice a day. I went to Ireland with a salmon rod, and caught nothing but the flu, which with great persistence I tried to cure by stopping in every country pub my bicycle happened to come across. That I sometimes don't catch the fish I originally seek is not surprising; that I no longer pretend to care is beginning to worry my friends.

But this was my third trip to Costa Rica. All frivolities should have long since been dispensed with. I had planned and researched and tied these beautiful artificial lures in preparation, and had even contacted a magazine and laid my intentions clearly on the line: I was going to try to set the new International Game Fish Association world record on Pacific sailfish. In other words, I was determined. In further words, I had a written contract.

So I landed in San José, Costa Rica, on a Thursday, with sincere intentions of being at one of the isolated billfishing camps on the Pacific coast by Friday night. Come Saturday, though, I was still in San José roaming the streets, getting lost, dickering badly in the marketplaces, and generally having a very good time.

San José is as different from most other Central American cities as Costa Rica is different from other Central American countries. First off, San José has one of the lowest crime rates in the world for a major metropolitan area. It's clean, too. You fly in through clouds and there, surrounded by mountains, is this great glittering city looking maybe a little bit like Atlanta, but without the freeways and Yuppie housing. Then, you walk out early and the *tienda* keepers are washing the sidewalks, and kids with pretty faces are holding hands on the way to school; there are fruit carts on every corner, the smell of sliced mangoes and pineapples mixing with the mountain air and the bakery smell of morning. The boundaries of the city, this metropolis of 800,000, seem to draw in then, and it becomes a personable and reasonable place not nearly so large as it actually is. Men and women smile at you; passersby shake your hand as you ask directions, then shake it again once you're thoroughly confused. It is a noisy, cheerful place, a city of country markets, ornate architecture, and Spanish formality. The people take great pride in the way they dress, and neither wearing shorts nor drinking beer in public is acceptable—unless you're an American, in which case misbehavior is not only expected, but greeted with wry looks, as if to say, "Ah, those crazy gringos . . ."

Anyway, it's one of the few cities where I'm tempted to linger, and I did. It was at the Key Largo, a bar where world expatriates and some of the most beautiful women in Costa Rica sometimes meet for pleasure and business (respectively), that I met Archie Fields, the owner and president of Río Colorado Lodge. Fields, a huge, articulate man in a guayabera shirt, was saying, "So, why just fish the Pacific coast? I can fly you up to my place; fish for tarpon or snook, the best in the world."

There was this really stunning brown-eyed girl smiling at me from across the room; and a man named Jack, wearing a silk scarf and one of those French kind of caps, was singing "Satin Doll" with a jazz band backup; and I think I told Fields I didn't want to catch tarpon and snook because I had Guides' Disease, only I'm not sure if he knew what that meant.

"You can fish for the jungle fish, then," he said. "Guapote and ma-chaca—you don't have those in Florida. They hit like bass and fight like tarpon. And you'll be our guest; won't have to pay for a thing."

This girl, whose name turned out to be Teresa, was winking now, and people were dancing because Jack had asked them to. I think I told Fields about my determination to set the world record on Pacific sail, but I'm almost certain I didn't tell him I'd always tried to avoid fishing resorts because most of them cater to Americans and seldom have much in common with the country in which they operate. Not only that, there was a question of ethics. No journalist with integrity accepts a freebie.

Fields said: "You can spend a couple days on the Caribbean. Head over to the Pacific later and get your sail." Then he leaned forward as if to share a secret. "If you really want to see this country, I can stick you in a boat, take you 70 miles upriver through some of the most beautiful rain forest in the world, have them drop you at the lodge."

So much for integrity, I left for Río Colorado the next morning.

○ ○ ○

I caught the boat in Moín, just east of Limón, after a drive through the mountains that lie between San José and the Caribbean—a car trip of remarkable beauty through cloud forests with silver rivers that roll toward valleys in the far distance. Then it was seven hours aboard, traveling a watercourse of rivers and canals northward that is the only means of commerce along Costa Rica's wilderness Mosquito Coast. The JUNGLE ADVENTURE sign atop Fields's open boat gave me pause at first, but then the forest began to crowd in, the river narrowed, and soon the method of conveyance no longer mattered. The canopy trees of the jungle—tropical moist forest by definition—grew and joined, 150 feet high, and the understory growth filled in, absorbing light, so that it seemed we were traveling through sheer, green canyons of tangled vines and bright flowers. Then the jungle would thin abruptly, coconut palms and banana thickets would appear, and there would be a few bamboo huts with pigs rooting beyond the swept lawns and with clothes dangling on the line, and children would come running toward us, grinning. Behind, dugout canoes would thrash on our wake.

Far to the north, only about 25 miles from the Nicaraguan border, we entered Tortuguero National Park, a preserve (inspired largely by the work of Archie Carr of the University of Florida) to protect the green turtle, which annually lays its eggs along the 22-mile stretch of beach there. The rain forest beyond, the most spectacular we had seen, is protected, too—and to Costa Rica's credit. Even so, Costa Rica's unprotected natural resources suffer from the very things that make the country attractive to travelers: nearly 40 years of political stability, and a much longer history of middle-class majority rule—a social oddity among the bitter caste fighting that keeps the rest of Central America in endless turmoil. Because Costa Rica is stable, outside corporations have invested here with confidence, including several American fast-food chains that now consider Costa Rica their major source of cheap beef. To increase production, corporations, individual ranchers, and Japanese logging contractors are expanding pasturage by leveling the rain forest at a phenomenal rate. It is said to take 15.2 square meters of pastureland to produce just a single quarter-pound hamburger patty, and it comes down to trading one of the world's greatest natural wonders for Big Macs and Whoppers. Riding a boat through the heart of it all, it seemed particularly nauseating to think that, at the present pace of destruction, 80 percent of Costa Rica's rain forests will be gone by the end of the century.

O   O   O

Río Colorado Lodge is a series of cabins connected by roofed boardwalks, all built on the edge of the Río Colorado and raised on pilings so that it seems you are staying on a huge raft, or maybe in a tree house. Lodge capacity is 24, but there were only about a dozen other guests when I arrived, most of them fishermen, but a few had come just for the river trip and to see the wildlife. I gravitated toward the latter group not because I don't like fishermen—I do—but because I don't like the specific brand of ego-brittle, blood-sport, name-dropping, would-be Hemingways that the former group seemed to be, heart and soul.

Sitting in the bar that first night with a nice couple from Boston, we overheard this conversation:

"I'd always thought the African elephant was dangerous until I came up against my first Cape buffalo. For my money, they're the most dangerous game going." (Pause for effect.) "I had to kill three of them just to be sure." (Laughter.)

Second man: "Yeah, but for action, you ever go shooting down in Columbia? They got this valley south of Bogotá that the farmers plant. I killed 466 dove there in one day. A *single* day. I'd of killed more, only my gun broke."

Third man: "Course, we carried $5,000 worth of shells with us— not everyone can do that."

No kidding, they said all that. It seems unlikely to me that lodges like Río Colorado get a steady flow of these people, probably because they show up so rarely on my charter boat. One of the great myths of chartering is that the people you take out are drunken boobs who pay big money to offend and to make fools of themselves. Just the opposite is true. Most of the people I take out are nice, some have become close friends over the years, and the fly-fishermen invariably know more about the sport's finer points than I do. But when you do get a bad group, it's almost always made up of blow-dried nimrods who pack the Gold Card in their wallets and gonads on their sleeves. That one of these jerks was a newspaper fishing writer from New Jersey, a guy who hung with the highfliers by trading free advertising for free trips, didn't do anything to buoy my spirits—especially because I was now doing exactly the same thing. The one bright spot that first night was that it had begun raining nonstop with no end in sight, and there was the very real possibility I wouldn't have to fish at all.

But then I met Rudy Dodero. Dodero, in his late twenties, was just back from playing soccer, and it looked as if fisticuffs had been involved. ("In theeese jungle we don't have soccer teams, we have soccer *armies.*") While he cleaned off the mud and blood, he outlined his life as freely as if I were his analyst—and it all revolved around fishing: fishing as a child growing up in Costa Rica, skipping school for fish tournaments, fishing on his honeymoon, now fishing on his time off from a job that was fishing. Some might have interpreted all this as extreme dedication, but I saw it for what it was and couldn't have been happier. After meeting Dodero, casting for bats seemed the natural progression on a path mutually shared. It was, in fact, a little bit like coming home.

○ ○ ○

Not only are there bats and fish in Costa Rica, but there are 820 species of birds—more than in the United States and Canada combined—plus a long list of Central American mammals and reptiles. This is all the more attractive because Costa Rica is a tiny country, smaller than West Virginia, and the zones of fauna demarcation—while they vary greatly and change abruptly—are never more than a few hours from one another. On a busy day you can watch iguanas and howler monkeys on the Pacific coast, fish for rainbow trout in the central mountains (some are more than 12,000 feet high), see quetzals in the cloud forests, then travel down into the Caribbean lowlands to look for three-toed sloths and American crocodiles.

I saw my first three-toed sloth during the car trip from San José to Moin, a pathetic, oil-stained creature crossing a busy highway. This animal moved into traffic with such mechanical resolve, like a windup toy with dying batteries, that it seemed less like a living creature than road kill on the hoof. I turned away and couldn't look back.

Batfishing in the Rainforest

I had seen a number of other native species at the zoo in San José, but it was on the Río Colorado that the diversity of the country's wild-life hit me full force. Fishing for machaca, we would run far upriver, cut the engine, then drift along a solid forest wall, casting poppers toward the bank. The silence would grow, then slowly freshen with sound: water dripping from the giant elephant-ear leaves, the wood-wind cry of a bird, a distant grunt followed by the frantic chatter of creatures unseen and unknown—all of this echoing for a moment, then quickly absorbed by the forest. Even with no wind, there was the steady groan of limbs and vines, the sound of the jungle itself, as if it were growing as you watched, and might, if you lingered, entangle and then consume you.

Spider monkeys would sometimes come rustling through the canopy, whole families of them, flushing parrots and green-billed toucans as they traveled to see the intruders who had come by boat. The females would stay to the rear, sometimes with babies clinging to their backs, while the males cautiously swung to the outer ledge of forest, their startlingly human eyes peering out. On the banks, turtles and crocodiles sunned themselves, and I saw several more sloths in the lower trees, each looking like a hairy, squint-eyed child. The most striking creatures amid all this activity, though, were the butterflies. They would come fluttering into the river gloom, catch a stray ray of light, and burst into bright flames of iridescent lavender or gold, then veer back into the shadows, the light still clinging to their wings.

To me, this was the best of fishing: being on the river in silence, the familiar weight of fly rod in hand, each cast serving as a kind of conduit by which you are not only linked to the quarry you seek, but, in moments of absolute concentration, rendered a legitimate extension of the river itself.

There were other good moments at Río Colorado. One night I crossed the fence separating the lodge from the village beyond and went to Mass, for it is my habit while traveling to attend whatever church is available. My reasons for doing this are more social than

spiritual, for there are no strangers in a small church, and as an outsider you are credited with virtues not normally ascribed to you by
friends who know the truth. On this night, though, I'd gotten the time
wrong because of my terrible Spanish, and no one was there. I left
money for the candle I'd lit, then sat in the plywood chapel and
watched as the village kids poked their noses over windowsills and
around corners, giggling at this silly gringo to whom, only a few hours
earlier, they had so carefully explained the church schedule. Couldn't
these Americans get anything straight?

Back at the lodge, though, things weren't quite so pleasant. Some
of the fishermen were upset because of the constant rain and angry
because the fishing, under these less than ideal conditions, wasn't as
spectacular as they'd hoped. Sure, they'd each had tarpon strike, but
their group had landed only one. Where was the constant action they'd
read about in the fishing magazines? Most of the anger was aimed at
Dodero, and the fishermen were taking sly, invidious avenues to vent
it. That night at dinner, Rudy's wife asked one of the men if the diamond in his ring was real. Slightly offended, the man held the ring to
the light, recited the karat weight—the stone was the size of a goi-
ter—and said: "But I got a good deal; it only cost me 16."

It was a trap; I knew it. But there was nothing to do but listen. "Six-
teen hundred dollars?" asked Rudy, amazed that someone could afford
to pay so much for a ring, but a little uncomfortable, too, because
Costa Rica is a poor country and open talk of big money is obviously
a subject of embarrassment.

The man bored in. "No, $16,000. I have a friend who's a jeweler if
you're interested."

Rudy and his wife winced visibly. He had told me what his salary
was, and it would take him three years to make that much money—a
fact the man with the ring had to at least suspect.

Despite all this, Dodero and his staff remained models of diplo-
macy, but I knew the complaining and the baiting had to be taking a
toll—for it was already wearing on me, a kind of sympathetic re-

sponse. The rain wouldn't stop, and the men weren't landing enough fish, and it was everyone's fault but their own. It is exactly this pressure to control the uncontrollable that is the spoor of Twig Syndrome, and I was feeling the familiar roll of stomach and abdominal tightness that, under different circumstances, I might have written off as nothing more than liver disease. Even worse for Rudy, this was all happening in plain view of a journalist—me.

I left the next day, insisting I had to get on with my quest for a world-record Pacific sail. But this was an excuse, a fiction that, if not dropped upon my arrival in San José, I had certainly abandoned now.

○ ○ ○

Tell some people you're going to Central America to fish, and you get this weird look, like maybe next time it will be mushroom hunting in Libya. Isn't it dangerous? they want to know. Don't the contras maintain bases in Costa Rica? The week before my arrival, there had been an explosion outside the U.S. Embassy, and the newspapers were filled with it. When I got back to San José, I decided to go to the embassy and ask just how dangerous it was roaming around this country. Costa Rican national guardsmen (Costa Rica dissolved its army in 1948 and funneled the money into education) gave me hard stares as I approached, and I passed through the door to find a U.S. Marine looking at me through bulletproof glass. Behind him, hanging on the wall, was a flak jacket, an M-16, and a large photograph of a smiling Ronald Reagan.

"You want to know about the explosion, sir? Went off across the street. Broke some glass, that's about all. It was just a grenade."

"Just a grenade?" I felt silly now that I'd even asked.

The Marine had short blond hair and big arms with veins showing—the kind of guy you like to see on the other side of something bulletproof. "Right. Just a grenade. That's about the only trouble we've had. The State Department advisories tell you to use common sense around the Nicaraguan border."

"So it's safe to travel anywhere else in the country?"

The Marine almost showed some emotion. "I don't know. You going by plane or driving?"

It was a point worth making. Put these kindly, mild-mannered Costa Ricans behind the wheel of a car, and some kind of bizarre personality transformation takes place. They become aggressive, wild, filled with a crazy faith in life after death. Various sources rate Costa Rica second or third in the world in per capita traffic accidents, and it seems a point of honor with them to someday be first. It's not the roads. The roads are generally very good and well maintained. It's the driving habits of the people, and I have no explanation for it. If you go to Costa Rica, forget about the contras and the Sandinistas—watch out for the Toyotas.

Riding on a crowded bus from San José to the Pacific, I saw fast rivers that certainly held trout, forests growing green in the mountain clouds, but all I could think of were these cars we kept meeting head-on as we passed slower vehicles on hills and curves. I pictured the police rooting through the inevitable carnage, finding my two beautiful fly reels—a handmade Sea Master and a big-game Fenwick—and kicking them into the ditch as nothing more than gold-plated cylinder heads.

Puntarenas, a Pacific port town dirty by Costa Rican standards, seemed almost pristine on arrival, a place where you might stumble off a bus and kiss the good earth. I got an inexpensive hotel room (the farther you get from San José, the cheaper everything is), then made the rounds of the fishing docks, looking for a boat to charter for sailfishing. Strangely, once shed of the pressure to fish for sails, it suddenly seemed like a fun thing to actually try. But the few boats operating were already booked, and the ones not booked were broken-down. I could have gone on up the coast to fishing resorts like Tamarindo Beach or El Ocotal, but that would have required a decision with hard edges and a certainty of purpose I not only lacked but didn't want very much. Instead, I settled on the Peninsula of Nicoya, a remote shoulder of mountains and wilderness beach that extends far out into the Pacific and where, it was said, whales came in close to shore and, in certain isolated areas, there were no sportfishing boats of any kind.

O O O

Peninsula of Nicoya: abrupt green hills with birds of paradise and bananas growing wild, the swept lawns of isolated villages connected by one-lane dirt roads more often traveled by horses than by cars. I stayed on the southeastern cusp of the peninsula, Bahía Ballena, at La Hacienda, a cattle ranch reminiscent of television's Ponderosa, but with the ocean out front and the mountains at its back.

Several years ago the owner of La Hacienda decided to build a few guest rooms, and now it has become a kind of bunkhouse-style hotel. The main house is constructed of heavy wood and red tile, with broad porches, hammocks, and grounds so perfectly kept that it's as if someone had transported a botanical garden to the seventh fairway of the Augusta Country Club. There are the hedges of hibiscus, in big red bloom, where hummingbirds compete with bees, and there are the coconut palms and mango trees with iguanas the size of dachshunds blinking beneath, and everywhere else you look there is nothing but water and vegetation and empty beach—unless you lean from your hammock enough to see the corrals, and then you can watch the cowboys branding or maybe doing rope tricks.

I fished there. I'd get up before sunrise, climb on a horse, and ride down the beach, a fly rod braced against my thigh like a Winchester. As the beach is the most convenient means of travel between the village of Pochote, three miles north, and the village of Tambor, three miles south, there were occasionally other solitary horsemen with whom to exchange waves, a pleasant thing in lonely country. I'd cast for a couple of hours, watching for the spout plumes of whales, then ride back, the sound of surf, the clatter of parrots, the eerie grunt and grumble of howler monkeys wild in the pale light.

At such times, La Hacienda seemed to be the best of Costa Rica, for

249

it afforded all those small intersections for which we travel—primitive backcountry and unaffected people—and there was the fishing, too, another form of intersecting, and with similar ends: to touch for a moment those kindred things of which you can never truly be a part. And sitting on the porch, one night at La Hacienda, reading by generator light, I was hardly even tempted when bats came vectoring down— fruit bats, maybe—called by the lamp's citreous glow in which, turning, I could see my fly rod against the rail, its golden reel glittering like something electrical, or something alive.